The Good, the Glad and the Funny

Political Jokes and Anecdotes

John Scally

BLACKWATER PRESS

Editor
Ciara McNee

Design & Layout
Paula Byrne

Cover Design
Karen Hoey

ISBN
1-84131-786-1

© 2005 John Scally

Produced in Ireland by
Blackwater Press
c/o Folens Publishers
Hibernian Industrial Estate
Tallaght
Dublin 24

Contents

Acknowledgements

Thanks to Bertie Ahern, Mary Banotti, Séamus Brennan, Proinsias De Rossa, Jim Glennon, Charles Haughey, Cian Hogan and Dick Spring for their stories.

While this book was being written, I was shocked and saddened to hear the news of the sudden death of Seán Doherty. He was great company and a gifted storyteller and will be much missed, especially in Roscommon.

Thanks to John O'Connor, Margaret Burns and all at Blackwater Press for their support for this book.

Dedication

To my new nephew Harry Minogue

Introduction

A little boy went to his dad and asked, 'What is politics?'

The dad thought for a while, and then said, 'Well, son, let me try to explain it like this. I'm the breadwinner of the family, so you could call me Capitalism. Now think about your mam – she's the administrator of the money, so we'll call her the Government. Your mam and I, we're here to take care of your needs, so we'll consider you to be the People. Your nanny works very hard, so we'll call her the Working Class. And lastly, your baby brother – let's call him the Future. Now, think about that and see if it makes sense.'

So the little boy went to bed and spent all evening thinking about what his dad had told him.

Later that night, the boy heard his baby brother crying and got up to check on him. He found that the baby had dirtied his nappy. The little boy went into his parents' room and found his mother sound asleep. Not wanting to wake her, he went instead to the nanny's room. Finding the door locked, he looked through the keyhole. To his surprise, he saw his father in bed with the nanny. The little boy gave up trying to wake anyone and went back to bed.

The next morning, the little boy said to his father, 'Dad, I think I understand the concept of politics now.'

The father replied, 'Good, son, tell me in your own words what you think politics is all about.'

The little boy said, 'Well, while Capitalism is screwing the Working Class, the Government is sound asleep. The People are being ignored and the Future is in deep poo.'

If the above story gives too jaundiced a classification of politics, perhaps a more academic definition is required. Etymologists have listed the two root words of the word 'politics'. The first is '*pol*' from '*polus*', meaning much or many. The second is 'tick', meaning any of numerous small, bloodsucking parasites which transmit diseases.

Politicians are interested in people. Not that interest is always a virtue. Fleas are interested in dogs. I met a Cork man the other day who told me that he was walking through a graveyard and came across a headstone that read, 'Here lies a politician, a true and honest man'. The Corkonian said to me, 'Wasn't it strange that they buried two people in the one grave!'

We live in an era in which transparency is expected of the political classes. Accordingly, I should declare my own biases and prejudices. I admit it – I like politicians. Researching this book has caused me to change my beliefs. Before this I didn't approve of political jokes. I have seen too many of them get elected.

Politics thrives on gossip. But what many people don't realise is that politics actually created gossip. Early politicians needed to know what the local people considered to be important. Since there were no telephones, TVs or radios, the politicians sent their assistants to local taverns, pubs and bars. They were told to 'sip some ale' and listen to people's conversations and political concerns. Many assistants were sent at different times. 'You go sip here' and 'You go sip there'. The two words 'go' and 'sip' were eventually combined and, thus, we have the term 'gossip'.

To the outsider, politics is a strange sport created by God on a bad day to pay humankind back for all its crimes. To the devotee it is an obsession. Inspiring as it does such extremes of love and hate, politics is the ideal breeding ground for high comedy, albeit mostly unintentional.

Many of the stories in this collection are strange but true. However, the veracity of some of the stories would not measure up to that expected in a court of law. They are based on real events. Only the facts have been changed! Many of these tales of the unexpected are shamelessly apocryphal. They are not meant to be statements of fact, but are intended to give a laugh or at least bring a smile. There are times when I have gone for the Dorothy Parker approach: 'I don't care what is written about me so long as it isn't true.'

In theory, politics is a theatre in which an attempt is made to take the superior position. In practice, it is often the forum where an engaging battle of wits occurs, with the electoral fight momentarily the last thing on anyone's mind. Sometimes the results are bemusing. More often, as we shall see, they are amusing.

It is said that humour and good taste are contradictions in terms. That is particularly the case with political humour. If you love political correctness, this is not the book for you. Hopefully, though, it is the book for those who love politics.

It was Oscar Wilde who pointed out that no comment was in bad taste if it was amusing. Quentin Crisp wrote: 'There are three reasons for becoming a writer: the first is that you need the money; the second that you have something to say that you think the whole world should know; the third is that you can't think what to do with the long winter evenings.' I would like to think that a fourth reason is to provide readers with something to do on the long winter nights. In a small way, this book attempts to celebrate the fun that is attached to politics and to give people a laugh or two.

Chapter 1 The Boss

Charlie Haughey stands alone on the Irish political landscape. Not since the Civil War has any Irish political figure been the source of such heated controversy. Haughey's career had more twists and turns than a bad bog road. It was enough to make a Greek dramatist leap in his sandals. In December 1979, Haughey achieved his longstanding ambition of being elected leader of Fianna Fáil and Taoiseach. He had mixed fortunes as Taoiseach, possibly because, as the late *Irish Times* journalist John Healy shrewdly observed, 'He was as cursed in his friends, as he was blessed in his enemies'. Haughey's has not been a quiet retirement, as news has emerged of his 'unusual financial arrangements'. Then Terry Keane brought her 'Keane Edge' to bear on his love life. This whole book could be filled with all the stories and rumours that have circulated about Charlie. I have selected just a tiny sample.

Self-evaluation

From time to time, Charlie has shown a nice line in self-deprecation. He admits that: 'Deep down, I'm a very shallow person.' Charlie always claimed to have one regret in his life: 'To my dying day, I'll regret that I was born too late for the permissive society.'

CJH was not known for his royalist sympathies, so people were surprised that he appeared to be getting on well with a royal at the Horse Trials in Punchestown in 1991. Asked what he had discussed with Princess Anne over dinner, Charlie replied, 'The menu'.

As Taoiseach, Charlie professed surprise at the state of the state's health service, even though the whole country knew it was in crisis. His Health Minister Rory O'Hanlon leaped to his defence with the immortal line, 'Waiting lists are a very unreliable measure of the availability of hospital services'.

Throughout his political career, Charlie attracted great hostility. One of his most famous critics was Conor Cruise O'Brien, who famously said, 'If I saw Mr Haughey buried at midnight at a crossroads with a stake through his heart – politically speaking – I would continue to wear a clove of garlic around my neck, just in case.'

In the 1980s, Charlie's political enemies seemed about as effective as a feather in a tornado. However in his later years as Taoiseach, Charlie's biggest enemies were his former friends Albert Reynolds and Pádraig 'Pee' Flynn. Pádraig once said, 'I'm not a vindictive person. Now people might say I'd cut your throat with barbed wire, but I'm not deliberately vindictive.' As a heave was planned against Haughey in 1982, Albert Reynolds was asked for a comment. He replied, 'Let's not speculate on the speculators.'

Charlie resigned as Taoiseach on the 11 February 1992. His final exchange in the Dáil was with Fine Gael TD Paddy Sheehan.

Sheehan: 'A Cheann Comhairle, seeing that the Taoiseach is departing his high office within the next few hours, before he goes I want to put the records of this house straight. When is the Taoiseach going to extend the powers of the Castletownbere Harbour Master over the waters of the Bearhaven Sound?'

An Ceann Comhairle: 'Deputy Sheehan, you're out of order, resume your seat or leave the house.'

Sheehan: 'Can't you see that the Taoiseach is on his feet and he's ready to answer?'

Haughey: 'Deputy Sheehan, the battle between us is now over, we will return our swords to the scabbards.'

After his retirement from politics, Charlie Haughey's biggest enemy became the Revenue Commissioners. Nonetheless, it is not true that he is so worried about the taxman that, when he pays you a compliment, he asks for a receipt.

Drink up

Back in the 1960s, Haughey was canvassing in Cavan. He got a bit thirsty and went into a pub. There was no one there and he rapped on the counter. The publican, who was having his lunch, appeared and got the whiskey that Charlie ordered. Then he went back to his meal. Charlie realised that he hadn't got any water with his whiskey and rapped again. This time the publican's little daughter came. 'I'd like some water for my whiskey,' Charlie said.

'Oh, you don't have to worry about that,' replied the little girl, 'I saw Daddy putting some in the bottle this morning.'

Straight talking

In 1980, Margaret Thatcher met Charlie Haughey and the then Minister for Foreign Affairs, Brian Lenihan, in 10 Downing Street. As always, Charlie had insisted that a gift be brought for Mrs Thatcher. There is a long-established protocol that on such occasions gifts are not given during the visit but presented in a short ceremony afterwards. As the Irish politicians entered the home of the British Prime Minister and were doing the round of handshakes with Mrs T and the officials, Charlie whispered softly to his minister, 'Have you got the gift?'

Lenihan replied with the softest whisper, 'The protocol, Taoiseach.'

Charlie whispered a little more loudly, 'Have you got her gift?'

Again Brian replied with the most delicate whisper, 'The protocol, Taoiseach.'

The affair was resolved when Charlie glared, as only he could, at his cabinet colleague and blurted out for all to hear: 'Give her the f****** present.'

If I were a rich man

During his time as Taoiseach, Haughey made many public pronouncements about the need for fiscal responsibility. Charlie doled out the following advice to the then southern correspondent of *The Irish Times*, Dick Hogan: 'Never worry about money – especially when you don't have it.'

Charlie's willingness to accept money from big business has been well documented. However, his generosity to others is often forgotten. When his home on his private island off the Kerry coast was being decorated, he arranged for a keg of Guinness for the builders. However, renovating the house proved to be very thirsty work. After the Guinness was finished, the lads decided to investigate Charlie's famed wine cellar, which had been lovingly and painstakingly stocked with expensive brands such as Haut-Brion. The vintage wine proved very palatable to the builders and they embraced the task of sampling it with gusto. To their horror after a few days of drinking, they found that that they had entirely exhausted Charlie's wine cellar. Knowing the pride that Mr Haughey took in his wine, the builders thought that they were in big trouble. Like all Kerry people, they were a resourceful bunch. The lads went to the local Spar on the mainland and bought every bottle of Blue Nun in the shop and used it to restock the cellar.

It fell to the Taoiseach's private secretary to break the calamitous news to Charlie. The poor civil servant was very nervous, and expected Charlie to eat him alive. Instead, when he heard of the builders' ingenuity, Charlie collapsed into fits of laughter.

Acquired wisdom

CJH is very knowledgeable about horses and very affable when attending race meetings. He was once asked for a tip. He replied, 'Life is too short to drink bad wine!'

Setting the record straight

Haughey remains a keen horseman, despite a few famous falls. It is alleged that he chose black and blue as his hunting colours because he was bruised so often after riding mishaps. When I quizzed him about the veracity of that remark, he laughed and gave a characteristically dismissive hand gesture. 'I think you'd have to take that as apocryphal!'

The roll of the dice

Charlie had an unusual management style. After he replaced Jack Lynch as Taoiseach in 1979, Charlie made sweeping changes to the cabinet. He called a Jack Lynch supporter into his office and handed him a dice and told him to throw it on the desk saying: 'Roll between a one and five and you're dropped from the cabinet.'

'What if I get a six?' asked the Lynch loyalist.

'You get another throw.'

The end is nigh

Around the same time, Haughey was having a chat with a TD who realised that he was entering the twilight of his ministerial career – but the end was coming faster than he had hoped: 'I'm confused, I don't know whether I'm coming or going,' the TD said.

'My friend,' Charlie replied, 'I can help you there – you're going.'

Stating the obvious

In the early 1980s, Charlie Haughey and some of his ministers were relaxing watching television when another member of the cabinet walked in. Pointing to the TV he asked: 'Who's that?'

Charlie replied, 'Mikhail Gorbachev.'

'What does he do?'

'He's the leader of the Soviet Union.'

'What's that on his head?'

'It's a birthmark.'

'How long has he had it?'

Icy comment

Early in 1981, Charlie called a brainstorming meeting of the cabinet to come up with ideas to boost the economy. In typical fashion, he pointed out flaws in several ambitious schemes set forth by his cabinet colleagues. 'Damn it, Charlie,' one said finally, 'do you have to throw cold water on everything?'

'Cold water,' countered Haughey, 'naturally results when a lot of hot air gets on thin ice!'

Heave-ho

Former Minister for Agriculture Jim Gibbons famously took the opposite side to Haughey during the Arms Trial. During one of Gibbons's heaves against Charlie in 1982, a supporter of Gibbons asked: 'What do you call Charles J. Haughey up to his neck in sand?'

Then, he answered his own question: 'Not enough sand.'

Charlie's day off

When Haughey was a schoolboy at St Joey's in Fairview, Dublin, he decided to mitch for the day. To ensure he would not subsequently face disciplinary measures, he decided to ring the school. He spoke to the secretary on the phone: 'I'm calling to report that Charles J. Haughey is unable to make it to school today because he is sick.'

The school secretary replied, 'I'm sorry to hear that. I'll note his absence. Who is this calling please?'

'This is my father.'

The meejah

During his time as Taoiseach, Charlie had to put up with a frequently hostile media. He became so cheesed off by the persistent media bashing that he decided to get away from it all for a sun holiday. One day, he took a break from sunbathing and went into a hi-tech electrical store to buy a car radio. The salesman said, 'This is the very latest model. It's voice-activated. You just tell it what you want to listen to and the station changes automatically. There's no need to take your hands off the wheel.'

When Charlie returned to Ireland, he had the radio installed. One evening, as he was driving to meet a lady friend, he decided to test it. 'Pop,' he said and the sound of the Beatles filled the car. Next he tried 'Country' and instantly he was listening to Daniel O'Donnell. Then suddenly two pedestrians stepped off the pavement in front of him, causing him to swerve violently. 'F****** idiots,' the Taoiseach shouted. Then the radio changed to a documentary on the role of journalists in Irish politics.

The mother of all hangovers

In the 1960s, Charlie went to a salubrious London hotel and ordered a drink. He was charged just over £1, which was a lot of money at the time.

'£1 for a drink?' he said to the man who served him. 'It's a different set of bars you should be behind.'

Honest to God

An autograph collector sent a photograph of Charlie Haughey to the Taoiseach's office, requesting an autograph. Instead, he received a terse note of refusal from Charlie's secretary. The collector promptly sent another photograph with the statement that he had no personal interest whatsoever in possessing Haughey's autograph, but wished to obtain it to sell for profit. The photograph was returned signed by Haughey with the additional notation: 'Bravo! Such honesty deserves encouragement.'

Charlie was less generous when an egotistical writer of his acquaintance asked him if he had read his last book. Charlie replied, 'Oh, yes, I agree that it should be your last.'

Constituency matters

Haughey was a great constituency TD. Once, one of his constituents went to a psychiatrist. 'Doctor,' he said, 'Every time I get into bed I think that there's somebody under the bed, and when I get under it, I think there's somebody on top of it. I'm going crazy.'

'Just put yourself in my hands for a few years,' said the psychiatrist. 'Come to me once a month and I will cure you.'

'How much do you charge?' the man asked.

'£40 per consultation,' came the reply.

'I'll think about it,' the patient said.

The man never returned. The following Christmas, he met the psychiatrist on Grafton Street. 'Why didn't you come to see me again?' asked the psychiatrist.

'At £40 a visit! I went to Charlie Haughey and he cured me for nothing.'

'How did he achieve that?' the doctor queried.

'He told me to cut the legs off the bed.'

Write it down. It's a good one

When Haughey was opening a hospital, he was repeatedly heckled by a woman. He stopped and said to her, 'Madame, when I was here ten years ago, I think you caused me some trouble. I don't remember your face but your dress is familiar.'

Another time, Charlie was asked to comment on a very elegantly dressed and heavily made-up woman. He replied, 'It's a poor ground that needs so much top dressing.'

The end of days

Charlie was told that a young politician was getting married the following day. 'Congratulations, my boy,' said Haughey. 'I'm sure you will look back on today as the happiest day of your life.'

'But I'm not getting married until tomorrow,' protested the young politician.

'I know,' said Charlie.

The camera never lies

Charlie was having a bad day, but had to have his photograph taken by a press photographer. The photographer had a lot of trouble getting his subject to pose properly. Eventually, after much bickering, he was about to take the picture.

'Look pleasant for a moment,' said the photographer. 'Then you can be yourself again.'

Dining out

Charlie was less than impressed by some of the food on offer at an official reception. He made his feelings known to the chef: 'It's not often you get the soup and the wine at the same temperature.'

The Fianna Fáil tour bus stopped off at a roadside café during a long coach drive. Haughey complained to PJ Mara: 'I went into the kitchen here and, do you know, there isn't a single bluebottle in there. They're all married with kids.'

Charlie was even more irate when he tasted the food. He asked the chef: 'What do you do about salmonella?'

The chef replied: 'I fry it in a little batter.'

One morning in a hotel, Charlie was not satisfied with some of the food. He called over the waiter and said: 'These eggs are awful.'

The waiter casually replied: 'Don't blame me. I only laid the table.'

Later that evening, Haughey had another encounter with the same waiter. When the waiter came over to his table, Charlie told him that he wouldn't be ready to order until his friends arrived. The waiter sarcastically replied: 'Oh, you must be the table for two, Sir.'

One evening, Charlie was frustrated that he had to wait so long for his dinner to be served in a posh restaurant. When the meal finally arrived he said, 'You're the same fellow who took my order. Somehow, I expected a much older waiter.'

A few months later, Charlie attended a reception. Many giants of politics such as Justin Keating, Conor Cruise O'Brien, John Bruton, Garrett Fitzgerald and Albert Reynolds were also there. An old TD, who had a reputation of being an utter bore and whose opinion of his own extraordinary abilities was shared only by himself, approached Haughey. The old man looked around the room and asked, 'How many great politicians do you think there are in this room?'

'One less than you think,' Charlie replied.

Breast is best

When Haughey was appointed Minister for Health in 1977, he asked his civil servants to make suggestions as to how he could improve the nation's health. He was a bit surprised when he received the following suggestion in a memo: 'You should consider designating the month of August Breast-Feeding Awareness Month. It would be a good time for employers to review their policies relative to breast-feeding employees.'

Wee Daniel

Daniel O'Donnell has long been one of Ireland's most popular entertainers. However, he also has his critics and is the butt of some very cruel jokes. It is said that whenever Daniel gets into a taxi he is greeted by the comment, 'I'll be happy to take you anywhere you want as long as you promise not to sing.'

Charlie Haughey had a 'liking problem' with Garrett Fitzgerald –
he didn't. Before the 1987 general election when Garrett was
Taoiseach, Charlie stood outside Garrett's office and played Daniel
O'Donnell records. When asked why he had done such a thing,
Charlie replied, 'If that doesn't get him out of his office, nothing will.'

All is fair in love and elections

During that general election, Charlie and Garrett found themselves
next to each other in a restaurant in Mallow. Garrett turned to
Charlie and said, 'You know why I'm going to win this election?
Because of my "personal touch". For example, I always tip waitresses
really well and then ask them to vote for me.'

'Oh, really?' replied Charlie. 'I always tip them 10p and ask them
to vote for you.'

The last judgement

Charlie Haughey and Garrett Fitzgerald were killed by a powerful
lightning strike. They had to go to purgatory before they were
allowed into heaven. Charlie was walking along, arm in arm, with a
beautiful young Page Three girl when he met his old foe.

'Well!' said Garrett, 'I see you're getting your reward up here, while
you purge your sins.'

'She's not my reward,' said Haughey. 'I'm her punishment.'

Seeing red

The radio series *Scrap Saturday* immortalised PJ Mara as the hapless
assistant to Charlie Haughey. Mara once claimed that the importance
of good PR people can be traced back to biblical times. Picture the
scene:

Moses and his flock arrive at the Red Sea, with the Egyptians in
hot pursuit. Moses calls a staff meeting.

Moses: 'Well, how are we going to get across the sea? We need a
fast solution. The Egyptians are close behind us.'

The General of the Armies: 'Normally, I'd recommend that we
build a pontoon bridge to carry us across. But there's not enough
time. The Egyptians are too close to us.'

The Admiral of the Navy: 'Normally, I'd recommend that we build bridges to carry us across. But time is short.'

Moses: 'Does anyone have a solution?'

Just then, his public relations man raised a hand.

Moses: 'You! Do you have a solution?'

The PR Man: 'No, but I can promise you this: if you find a way out of this one, I can get you two or three pages in the Old Testament.'

Chapter 2 The Most Cunning

Groucho Marx famously said, 'Politics is the art of looking for trouble, finding it everywhere, diagnosing it incorrectly and applying the wrong remedies.' Since 1997, Bertie Ahern has dominated Irish politics. The late Jim Kemmy's verdict on Bertie has been vindicated, 'Beneath that gauche and artless exterior lies a steely politician.'

Bertie made his name as Minister for Labour in the 1980s, when he resolved many difficult industrial disputes. However, he was a little taken aback during a pay dispute when a trade unionist told him: 'Four per cent of nothing is nothing. We want 12 per cent.'

The Taoiseach has always had his priorities right. In 1998, Bertie told the *Evening Herald*, 'The only things I always have in my wallet are the St Francis Xavier Novena of Grace Prayer... and the Manchester United fixtures list.'

Bertie sometimes exhibits an ability to put his foot on the accelerator while leaving his brain in neutral. This often has interesting results for the English language. In 2001, Bertie made an unusual complaint about Fine Gael's economic policies: 'They are trying to upset the apple tart.'

Bertie has a sharper sense of humour than he is given credit for. He spoke at a function in Belvedere College, after Tony O'Reilly had given a lengthy address. Bertie began his speech by saying, 'I'd like to congratulate Belvedere College on the great job dey did in teaching Tony O'Reilly to speak so well. A pity dey didn't teach him to stop!'

A little morsel

'Now, Bertie,' the parish priest said to his young altar boy, Ahern, 'when the Archbishop arrives don't forget to say "Your Grace".'

The bell rang precisely at the appointed time. Bertie hurried to the door, opened it, looked at the Archbishop and solemnly said: 'Bless us, O Lord, and these Thy gifts, which of Thy bounty we are about to receive, through Christ our Lord. Amen.'

The gift

Early in his marriage Bertie lived by the adage: A man who forgets his wife's birthday will get something to remember her by. One year before they even got married, Bertie decided to buy Miriam a button-up cardigan for her birthday. Venturing into a small shop, he approached a salesgirl, but the word 'cardigan' suddenly escaped him. Faltering for only a moment, he managed to utter, 'I want a sweater for my girlfriend – one that unbuttons down the front.' Realising what he had said, he beat a hasty retreat out of the shop.

Dressed for the occasion

As the following story indicates, when Bertie first became Taoiseach he was not known for his sartorial elegance. Two elderly Americans were finally discovered in a disused Japanese POW camp, having been captured during World War II. They first asked their rescuers, 'How is President Roosevelt?'

'Oh, he died a long time ago.'

'And how is Stalin?'

'Oh, he died a long time ago?'

'Please tell us that Winston Churchill is still alive and well.'

'Alas, I'm afraid he died as well.'

'Tell us, is Bertie Ahern still wearing that same anorak?'

The numbers game

When he was Minister for Finance Bertie observed: 'There are three kinds of people in this world; those who can count and those who can't.'

School reunion

Bertie went to visit his old school, St Aidan's in Whitehall. He asked the students if anyone could give him an example of a 'tragedy'. One boy stood up and offered the suggestion that, 'If my best friend who lives next door was playing in the street when a car came along and killed him, that would be a tragedy.'

'No,' Bertie said, 'that would be an ACCIDENT.'

Another boy raised his hand. 'If the Manchester City team bus drove off a cliff, killing everybody involved…that would be a tragedy.'

'I'm afraid not,' explained Bertie. 'That is what we would call a GREAT LOSS.' The room was silent; none of the other children volunteered. 'What?' asked Bertie, 'Is there no one here who can give me an example of a tragedy?'

Finally, a boy in the back raised his hand. In a timid voice, he spoke: 'If an airplane carrying you and the cabinet was blown up by a bomb, that would be a tragedy.'

'Wonderful.' Bertie beamed. 'Marvellous. And can you tell me why that would be a tragedy?'

'Well,' said the boy, 'because it wouldn't be an accident, and it certainly would be no great loss.'

Spirits in the sky

During a Dáil debate, there was a lightning strike and both Bertie Ahern and Enda Kenny were sadly killed. The pair ascended into heaven and, given their status in the political hierarchy, they bypassed St Peter at the Pearly Gates. Bertie and Enda were brought in the VIP entrance and were greeted by no less than God himself. 'Greetings. Heaven is enriched by having both of you here. Come on and I'll show you your accommodation. I hope you'll both be comfortable.'

God took Bertie by the hand, and led him off on a short walk through fields of flowers, until they came across a pretty thatched cottage by a stream. It had a beautiful garden, lovely flower beds and tall trees swaying in the gentle breeze. Bertie was left uncharacteristically speechless. Eventually he muttered, 'I don't know what to say.'

God then took Enda up the path. As they were strolling away, Bertie looked around him. Further up the road, he saw a gigantic mansion, with massive pillars. The house and gardens were surrounded by stands of Fine Gael emblems. There were huge 20-foot-high golden statues of John Costello, Liam Cosgrave and Garrett Fitzgerald overlooking a magnificent garden. A little flustered, Bertie ran after God and his old rival and tapped God on the shoulder. 'Excuse me, God,' Bertie said, 'I don't wish to sound ungrateful or anything, but I was wondering why Enda's house is so much more stylish than mine.'

God smiled beatifically at him and said: 'There, there, Bertie, don't worry, it's not Enda's house. It's mine!'

Techno-speak

Bertie Ahern wanted to buy a CD player, but was completely perplexed by one model's promotional sign. So he called the salesperson over and asked, 'What does "hybrid pulse D/A converter" mean?'

To which the salesperson replied, 'That means that his machine will read the digital information that is encoded on CDs and convert it into an audio signal.'

'In other words,' Bertie said, 'this CD player plays CDs.'

'Exactly.'

Different perspectives

In the run up to the March 2005 by-election in Meath, Bertie Ahern and Enda Kenny inadvertently scheduled simultaneous campaign rallies in the same part of Navan. After a lengthy round of speeches, the party leaders and their candidates worked their way through the crowd, shaking hands, kissing babies and beaming mightily. Suddenly, the skies opened and it began to rain. Bertie fled to take shelter in a nearby pub along with his entire team. Enda, however, continued to move through the crowd, shaking hands and kissing babies.

'That man's persistence yonder,' observed one of the locals, 'sure makes it easy to know who to vote for.'

'Yep,' another native agreed. 'Sure, I can't see myself casting a vote for a man who hasn't the good sense to come in out of the rain.'

I have a dream

Bertie Ahern had a dream in which he met Seán Lemass. In the dream, Bertie asked, 'Seán, what can I do to make things better for the people?'

Lemass replied, 'Lower taxes.'

Bertie said, 'Oh, Seán, I can't do that.'

The next night, Bertie dreamed again but this time Jack Lynch was there. 'Jack,' Ahern said, 'what can I do to make things better for the public?'

Lynch replied, 'Lower the taxes.'

Bertie answered, 'You too? I can't do that.'

The next night, Bertie dreamed again, and this time Michael Collins was there. 'Michael, what can I do to make things better for the people?'

Collins thinks for a moment and says, 'Em…go in an open car to mBéal na Bláth.'

For whom

Bertie was in his constituency office in Drumcondra when the phone rang. He answered it and a male voice said, 'Come on over.'

Bertie replied, 'Sorry?'

The voice continued impatiently, 'Come on over. We're waiting for you.'

Bertie said, 'I think you might have the wrong number.'

Much annoyed, the voice asked, 'To whom I am speaking?'

There was a pause and then Bertie said, 'I'm sorry. You've definitely got the wrong number. Nobody I know says "whom".'

Bertie's principles

Bertie is famous for his apparent ability to speak out of both sides of his mouth at once. In April 2005, when one of his backbenchers was caught driving while drunk, Bertie was asked about his attitude to alcohol. Bertie replied, 'If you mean the demon drink that wrecks marriages and causes road accidents – I'm against it. But if you mean the source of Christmas cheer and many a good traditional music session or singsong, then I'm for it.'

Lady like

Bertie's daughter, Cecilia, has formally joined the Manchester United fan club. She got a letter from them which was addressed to 'C. Ahern Esquire'. Cecilia rang up the club and said: 'I'm not a man, I'm a lady.'

A few days later a letter arrived addressed to 'Lady C. Ahern'.

A skinful

It is always said that politicians need a thick skin. The Taoiseach is the living proof of this – metaphorically and literally.

A sudden transformation occurs in Ireland's most powerful man when he recounts the most memorable moment of his soccer career. He shifts uncomfortably in his chair, wincing at the memory. His eyes are deep pools of pain.

'In the early 1970s there was a few bob to be made in the summer seven-a-sides. Because of that it was a very serious business indeed. The cream of League of Ireland players were involved, like Ben Hannigan and Eric Barber. It was shortly before I got married and I was working as an accountant in the Mater Hospital. I didn't have time to go home for my gear. All I had was a pair of squash shorts with a fly and a zip. Disaster struck in the dressing-room. I got my foreskin stuck in my zip. I was in agony.' (The wounded tone of his voice leaves no room for doubt about the veracity of this claim.)

'There was a fella from Cork in the dressing-room called Barry. I can't remember his surname, but I will never forget him to my dying day. He had lived in America and served with the US Army in

Vietnam. At first he suggested that I go to the Mater, but there was no way I would agree to that because I worked there. Barry then rustled up a jar of Vaseline and a knife and went to work to untangle me…if that's the right term!'

The saga of the zip, Vaseline and the knife is not for the squeamish, nor for those about to eat. Suffice to say the delicate operation was completed successfully – if very painfully – and the future Fianna Fáil leader was spared the nickname Bertie Bobbit!

'I had taken part in the kick-about before the game and my team-mates had no idea why I didn't take my place on the pitch in the first half. They played on with six men, but I came back on for the second half. That's dedication for you! We won 2–1 but the lads never knew why I missed the first half.'

Deliver us from evil

On the basis of a recent opinion poll, *The Sunday Tribune* has predicted that Fianna Fáil will sustain significant seat losses in the next general election. Bertie has responded by turning to religion. He now begins and ends the day by saying the politicians' prayer: 'O, Lord, you have given us minds. You have given us mouths. Help us to keep the two connected.'

Deliver us from Eddie

The summer of 2005 was a miserable one for the career of Bertie Ahern. He was not helped by the antics of some of his colleagues like Conor 'Sleeping Beauty' Lenihan. However, the real bane of his life has been the people's champion, Eddie Hobbs. As a result of Eddie's campaign, the Taoiseach is fervently hoping the bottom will fall out of the nappy market.

Chapter 3 The Lynch Mob

At his peak, the late Jack Lynch was an even more popular Taoiseach than Bertie Ahern. Jack was famous for his rendition of 'The Banks'. Had he been alive today, then he – and not Finian McGrath – would have appeared on *Celebrity You're a Star*. Jack, Ireland's most famous pipe smoker, was a man of great serenity and wisdom. When a colleague confided to him that he was having marital problems, the Taoiseach puffed on his pipe and calmly said: 'Some men get what they deserve. Others remain bachelors.' Lynch was a great 'constituency man'. The only time he was stumped was when a woman approached and presented the following dilemma: 'I won't marry him when he's drunk. He won't marry me when he's sober.' Jack was reduced to silence.

Mon man

As a pupil at the famous North Mon, Lynch had a keen appreciation of the role of the Christian Brothers in Irish life in general, and in the promotion of hurling in particular. He especially admired their commitment and the commitment they inspired in others. He once told the story of a clever little boy at an expensive and liberal private school who was badly underachieving, particularly in maths. So his parents, devout atheists, sent him to a very strict Christian Brothers' establishment. The young boy returned after the first day, tiny schoolbag brimming with books, and locked himself in his room for three hours to do his homework. This went on for a few weeks, and at the end of his first month he returned with his interim report, which showed that he was first in his class in maths. His delighted parents asked what had awakened his drive, and he said, a bit grimly, 'I knew that it was a serious subject when they showed me the guy nailed to the plus sign!'

Jack was well able to tell stories against himself. One goes back to his schooldays. One day, his father said to him, 'Tell me, Jack, how did your test go today?'

'Well, I did just what Napoleon did.'

'And what's that?'

'I went down in history.'

From a Jack to a king

Before entering politics, Jack Lynch won five All-Ireland hurling medals with Cork. He also won an All-Ireland football medal. He has an enduring memory from the 1945 All-Ireland football final. Lynch took mischievous pleasure in recalling Frank O'Connor's claim that Cork has a mental age of 17 – you had to leave at 17 if you were to be happy and stimulated – whereas Dublin had a mental age of 21.

Jack had just completed his law examinations and was in 'digs' in Rathgar on the southside of Dublin. He met the Cork team at Kingsbridge (now Heuston) Station on the Saturday evening. He told the selection committee that he would not meet the team at the hotel the next morning, as there was a bus route near his digs which passed by Croke Park. On Sunday morning, he was waiting in a queue about 20 yards long. Bus after bus passed, each taking only a couple of people at a time.

When another bus pulled up at the stop, Lynch barged to the head of the queue. The conductor told him to go back and wait his turn. Jack pointed to his bag of togs and said he had to play in the All-Ireland football final in Croke Park within the hour. The conductor said sarcastically that that was the best reason for jumping a queue that he ever heard. Nonetheless, he let Jack on.

When Jack arrived at Croke Park, he ran around to the back of the Cusack Stand to the dressing-rooms. With about 15 minutes to the throw-in, he knocked on the Cork dressing-room door. All he could hear were footsteps slowly and deliberately pacing the floor. The door opened. It was Jim Hurley, chairman of the Cork Selection Committee. Lynch expected to be 'bawled' out. Instead he got, 'Hello Jack Lynch, you were great to come.'

The fear factor

One of Jack's most terrifying experiences was playing a county junior football final. The final was delayed due to the usual quota of objections about anything and everything. So by the time it was played, most of the better players had returned to college and were unavailable. Jack was drafted in to play at corner forward, even though he was only about 15 years of age. He became increasingly worried as he went to take up his position and saw a 'seasoned' cornerback advancing to meet him. Jack was getting more intimidated with each step but was puzzled when, at the last moment, the cornerback veered off from him and went back towards his goalkeeper. He took out his false teeth and loudly told his 'keeper: 'Paddy, mind these in case I forget myself and eat someone.'

Licence to thrill

Racing punters are notorious for their partisan stance. Jack once backed a horse at the Phoenix Park which led all the way and was 15 lengths clear at the end. He declared it to be the most thrilling finish he had ever witnessed.

Climbing the greasy pole

Lynch once joked, 'A good speech isn't one that proves that a Minister is telling the truth but one in which no one can prove he's lying.' He also enjoyed Oscar Levant's comment that, 'A politician will double cross that bridge when he comes to it.'

During the 1977 general election campaign, Jack went to an old folks home to canvas for votes. One woman had a bad-tempered face and her voice seemed remarkably like a dog growling. She insisted on telling the prospective Taoiseach her life story. She had recently gone to the dentist to have her false teeth adjusted for the fourth time but they still didn't fit.

'Well,' said the dentist, 'I'll do it again this time, but no more. There's no reason why these shouldn't fit your mouth easily.'

'Who said anything about my mouth?' she answered. 'They don't fit in the glass.'

The golden years

In later years, Lynch was occasionally asked to reflect on the ageing process. He loved George Burns's comment about turning 80: 'I can do all the things today I did at 18, which tells you how pathetic I was at 18.'

Lynch also enjoyed telling the story of the celebrated writer, Somerset Maugham. On reaching his 70th birthday, Maugham was invited to a celebratory dinner in London. As is usual on such occasions, he was obliged to make a speech. He reluctantly rose to his feet and having thanked all those he should have thanked, and hoping he hadn't forgotten those he had forgotten, he explained that there were many very positive advantages, comforts and solaces attached to the inevitable process of ageing. His guests, many of whom were of equal vintage, were naturally heartened by this piece of information. Then after a long silence, Maugham announced that he could not for the life of him think what they were.

A place in history

Another favourite Lynch story was the one about the TD who went to an auction to buy a valuable parrot. He badly wanted this parrot and thought of bidding up to £40. The bidding went up to £120 before it was knocked down to him. Afterwards he asked the auctioneer who the other man was who kept bidding against him. 'That wasn't a man; that was the parrot you bought,' replied the auctioneer.

Tact

After giving a speech in Cork, Jack Lynch was approached by a grandmotherly-looking woman, who told him how greatly she enjoyed his remarks.

'I was encouraged to speak to you,' she added, 'because you said you loved old ladies.'

'I do,' said the very gallant Jack, 'but I also like them your age.'

Chapter 4 They're Part of Who We Are

Like the Catholic Church and the GAA, Fianna Fáil occupies a special place in Irish life. The party stretches its tentacles into every parish in the country. Fianna Fáil has produced more than its fair share of 'characters', who have left an indelible imprint on the Irish political landscape – not always in the way Party HQ might have liked. This chapter celebrates some of the party's more memorable individuals. It is a guide or travelogue around the sometimes strange ways in which the biggest force in Irish politics does its business.

The Life of Brian

To many people, the late Brian Lenihan summed up the quintessential Fianna Fáil ethos. When he appeared on a special *Late, Late Show* tribute to him, Lenihan told jokes about his willingness to 'offer' gardaí transfers when they caught him and his political friends drinking after hours in the 1960s.

In the mid-1960s Lenihan was a member of the brash 'mohair suit' brigade of Fianna Fáil ministers who included Charles Haughey, Donough O'Malley, Neil Blaney and Seán Flanagan. He was always put on television whenever the party needed someone to defend the indefensible. His tactic was to speak off the point, or in his own words, use a 'policy of scientific confusion'. Accordingly, the late Fine Gael Minister John Kelly once described Lenihan as, 'the Minister for Bustle and Spoof'. Nonetheless, Lenihan was one of the most popular ever members of Dáil Éireann.

After sitting through a GAA club dinner during which speech after speech was made to the increasingly drunk audience, Brian was at long last invited by the Chairman to provide a short address. 'Athlone, Co. Westmeath,' he replied.

The top three

When he was Minister for Education, Brian was asked to speak to a group of school kids. At the end of his upbeat speech, he asked the boys whether they had any questions. A rather timid boy put up his hand and asked Brian whom he considered to be the three greatest Irish politicians of all time. Brian replied, 'Well, the other two were de Valera and Lemass.'

Another time, Brian went to open a school in Roscommon. He talked to some of the students and encouraged them to learn about other cultures and remarked, 'One half of the world is ignorant of how the other half lives.'

One little boy put up his hand and said, 'Not in this village, Sir.'

No jobs for the boys

A constituent approached Brian to see if he could get him a job as a caretaker in the local secondary school. The following week, the constituent returned to Brian's clinic but the Minister broke the bad news. 'I'm sorry, Jim, but they just couldn't find any work for you. They have barely enough for their present staff.'

'Ah,' said the man, 'sure the little bit I do won't make any difference.'

Bless me, Father

After another constituent became a father for the first time, Brian went to visit him and congratulate him personally on the achievement. When he returned home, Brian's wife asked him for a report. Brian replied, 'Baby flawless, mother breathless, father legless.'

Lord of the dance?

After a few drinks, Lenihan occasionally developed an exaggerated opinion of his prowess as a dancer. 'Dancing is in my blood,' he told his suffering partner at a Fianna Fáil fundraising dinner dance. 'You must have very bad circulation,' she replied.

Songs of praise

Canvassing for an election, Brian found himself in a convent talking about religion to a group of nuns. One sister lamented the decline in religious practice and the loss of the high standards of chastity which had prevailed in the 1950s. Brian remarked on the fact that there were more agnostics after television came to Ireland. One perplexed nun remarked with a sad sigh, 'I suppose we shouldn't be too hard on agnostics. After all there are many religions, but I suppose they all worship the same God.'

Strange blessings

When Brian lost his seat in Roscommon in the 1973 general election, a sympathiser said, 'It may well be a blessing in disguise.'

Brian replied, 'At the moment it seems quite effectively disguised.'

A house divided

In the early 1970s, Fine Gael leader Liam Cosgrave was having trouble with his internal critics in the party, whom he memorably dubbed the 'mongrel foxes'. Brian remarked, 'Fine Gael is like a stagecoach. On the odd occasion they can rattle along at great speed and everybody is too exhilarated or too carsick to cause any trouble. But once they stop, everyone gets out and argues where to go next.'

Forever friends?

In 1990, Charlie Haughey sacked Lenihan from the cabinet, after the latter's problems with 'mature recollection' during the presidential election. Nonetheless, the two had always been and remained very close, politically. After Haughey resigned as Taoiseach, Brian was the only TD to visit him in his office.

One of the many apocryphal stories told about Charlie dates back to the 1987 general election, when Brian sometimes accompanied him on his journey around the constituencies. They were up in a helicopter when a gust of wind nearly blew the roof off the machine. Charlie said, 'Brian if this turns upside down, will you and I fall out?'

Brian replied, 'No problem, Charlie, me and you will always be friends.'

For his part, Haughey also made a joke about the relationship. Asked if he had made his peace with Brian after sacking him, Charlie replied, 'Certainly. In fact he enjoyed my hospitality in Kinsealy yesterday. He came to my granddaughter's christening party. He wasn't invited but he came.'

Should old acquaintance be forgot

During a night on the town, Brian Lenihan was at the bar when he spotted someone he recognised from back home. He rushed up and greeted his 'friend' effusively: 'What brings you to Dublin?'

'I live here,' was the reply in a tone that, had Brian been less inebriated, would have told him that the man had absolutely no idea who the politician was.

'Didn't you used to have a beard at one time?' asked Brian.

'No.'

'You used to be taller. You must have shrunk, but it's great to see you all the same, Sam.'

'My name isn't Sam, it's Paul.'

'Good God! You've changed your name as well.'

Back to front

Priest: 'You are doing the Stations of the Cross backwards.'

Brian Lenihan: 'I thought there was something wrong alright, Father. Jesus seemed to be getting better!'

Abrakebabra

Brian's son Conor has inherited his father's capacity to make political ripples. After his notorious comments about Casa workers and kebabs in May 2005, a story did the rounds in Leinster House about Conor. His wife appeared on the popular ITV show *Who Wants to Be A Millionaire* with Chris Tarrant.

Chris: 'You're up to £500,000 with one lifeline left: phone a friend. If you get it right, the next question is worth £1 million. If you get it wrong, you drop back to £32,000. Are you ready?'

Mrs Lenihan: 'Yes.'

Tarrant: 'Which of the following birds does not build its own nest? Is it (A) robin, (B) sparrow, (C) cuckoo or (D) pigeon?'

Mrs Lenihan: 'I'd like to phone a friend. I'll call my husband, Conor.'

Conor answered the phone: 'Hello.'

Chris: 'Hello, Conor, it's Chris Tarrant from *Who Wants to Be a Millionaire*. I have your wife here, who needs your help to answer the £1 million question. The next voice you hear will be hers.'

Mrs Lenihan: 'Conor, which of the following birds does not build it's own nest: Is it (A) robin, (B) sparrow, (C) cuckoo or (D) pigeon?'

Conor: 'Oh, that's simple. It's a cuckoo.'

Mrs Lenihan: 'Are you sure?'

Conor: 'I'm sure.'

Chris: 'You heard Conor. Do you keep the £500,000 or play for the million?'

Mrs Lenihan: 'I want to play; I'll go with (C) cuckoo.'

Chris: 'Is that your final answer?'

Mrs Lenihan: 'Yes.'

Chris: 'Are you confident?'

Mrs Lenihan: 'Yes. Conor is very smart.'

Chris: 'You said (C) cuckoo, and you're right! Congratulations, you have just won £1 million!'

To celebrate, the Lenihans went to New York. On their first night there, they went to a posh restaurant. Mrs Lenihan gazed lovingly into Conor's eyes and asked him, 'Tell me, darling, how did you know that it was the cuckoo that does not build its own nest?'

'That's easy, everybody knows they live in clocks.'

A policy change

Conor Lenihan was holding open interviews in Leinster House for the position of office secretary. 'What's your name?' he asked the first man who showed up.

'John,' the new man replied.

Lenihan scowled, 'Look, I don't know what kind of namby-pamby place you worked in before, but I don't call anyone by their first name. It breeds familiarity and that leads to a breakdown in authority. I refer to my employees by their last name only – Smith, Jones, etc. That's all. I am to be referred to only as Mr Lenihan. Now that we have got that straight, what's your last name?'

The new man sighed, 'Darling. My name is John Darling.'

'Okay, John, the next thing I want to ask you is...'

Music to the ears

One evening, Conor Lenihan was babysitting his brother Brian's children. While his young nephew was practising the violin in the living-room, Conor was trying to read the paper in the kitchen. The family dog was lying beside him, and as the screeching sounds of the little boy's violin reached the dog's ears, he began to howl loudly. Conor listened to the dog and the violin for as long as he could. Then he jumped up, slammed his paper to the floor and yelled above the noise, 'For God's sake, can't you play something the dog doesn't know.'

Saving the day

Conor's aunt Mary O'Rourke has long been known for her quick wit. This was apparent at an early age when she appeared as Mary in a nativity play in Athlone. The play was unscripted. The children were given the bones of the story and then had to act it out, using their own words. All went according to plan until Joseph and Mary arrived at the inn. 'Have you any room for me and Joseph?' Mary asked.

The young boy playing the part of the innkeeper was a generous little man and nearly ruined everything by shouting back: 'We have plenty of room here, Mary, come on in and make yourself at home.'

Thankfully, little Mary was a fast thinker and saved the day by saying, 'Thanks all the same, John, but I've changed my mind. I think I'd rather stay at the stable down the road.'

No bread

In June 2005, the former Minister of Finance Charlie McCreevy listed his priorities to *The Sunday Business Post*. He said that the majority of people: '…wanted to earn a decent living, be able to afford a few pints, go to a football match and have a bit of sex.'

When he was six years old, Charlie McCreevy was in church. When the Communion was passed out, his mother leaned over and told him that he was not old enough to partake in the Eucharist.

When the collection basket was passed around, she leaned over once again to tell him to drop his sixpenny bit in. Charlie held his money firmly in his hand, stating, 'If I can't eat, I won't pay.'

Apples

When the young Charlie McCreevy first switched from Kill National School to CBS Naas, he went to the cafeteria for lunch. In the best tradition of the Christian Brothers, the boys were lined up patiently getting their lunches. At the head of the serving line was a large pile of apples. One of the Brothers had written a notice that said, 'Take only one, God is watching.'

Seeing this, Charlie wrote a notice of his own and placed it at the other end of the serving line, in front of a large pile of Fig Roll biscuits.

Charlie's note read: 'Take all you want, God is watching the apples.'

Feeling jumpy

One evening at 8.58 pm, Charlie McCreevy walked into a sports bar. He sat down next to a woman at the bar and stared up at the TV. The 9 o'clock news started. Charlie Bird was covering a story about a man on a ledge of a tall building preparing to jump.

The woman looked at Charlie and said, 'Do you think he'll jump?'

Charlie replied, 'You know, I bet he'll jump.'

The woman answered, 'Well, I bet he won't.'

Charlie placed €100 on the bar and said, 'You're on.'

Just as the woman placed her money on the bar, the guy did a swan dive off the building, falling to his death. The woman was very upset and handed her €100 to McCreevy, saying, 'Fair's fair. Here's your money.'

Charlie replied, 'I can't take your money, I saw this earlier on the 6 o'clock news and knew he would jump.'

The woman replied, 'I did too; but I didn't think he'd do it again.'

McCreevy took the money.

Skill

A local bar in a remote part of rural America was so sure that its bartender was the strongest man around that they offered a standing $1,000 bet. The bartender would squeeze a lemon until all the juice ran into a glass. Anyone who could squeeze one more drop of juice would win the money. Many people had tried over time but nobody could do it. One day Charlie McCreevy came into the bar and said softly, 'I'd like to try the bet.'

After the laughter had died down, the bartender grabbed a lemon, and squeezed away. Then he handed the wrinkled remains to Charlie. But the crowd's laughter turned to total silence as the Irish man clenched his fist around the lemon and six drops fell into the glass.

As the crowd cheered, the bartender paid the $1,000, and asked McCreevy, 'What do you do for a living? Are you a lumberjack, a weight-lifter, what?'

Charlie replied, 'I'm a Minister for Finance.'

Odds on

Charlie McCreevy is one of Irish racing's most devout patrons. Nonetheless, he has not gone so far as to liken himself to a horse — unlike former British Chancellor of the Exchequer Norman Lamont, who once commented: 'Desert Orchid and I have a lot in common. We are both greys; vast sums of money are riding on our performance; the opposition hopes we will fall at the first fence; and we are both carrying too much weight.'

A proper Charlie

During a long drive, McCreevy stopped alongside a field on a country road to rest a few minutes. He had just closed his eyes when a horse came to the fence and began to boast about his past.

'Yes, Sir, I'm a fine horse. I've run in 25 races and won over €2 million. I keep my trophies in the barn.'

Charlie computed the value of having a talking horse, found the horse's owner and offered a handsome sum for the animal.

'Aw, you don't want that horse,' said the farmer.

'Yes I do,' said McCreevy, 'and I'll give you €100,000 for him.'

Recognising a good ideal, the farmer said without hesitation, 'He's yours.'

While he wrote out his cheque, Charlie asked, 'By the way, why wouldn't I want your horse?'

'Because,' said the farmer, 'he's a liar – he hasn't won a race in his life.'

A misunderstanding

While they were cabinet colleagues, Maire Geoghegan-Quinn and Pádraig Flynn went into a restaurant to discuss how they might oust Charlie Haughey as Taoiseach and replace him with Albert Reynolds. As they read the menu, the waitress came over and asked Pádraig, 'Are you ready to order?'

Flynn replied, 'Yes, I'd like a quickie.'

The waitress nearly fainted.

Maire immediately leaned over to Pádraig and said, 'For God's sake, Pádraig, it's pronounced quiche.'

What a shower

During an appearance on *The Late, Late Show* Pádraig Flynn famously boasted about the number of houses he owned and complained about how hard it was to maintain all of them. When he became European commissioner and was setting up home in Brussels, he brought his wife to a bathroom-supply store. They discussed their needs with a young saleswoman. Since it was near closing time, they had to curtail their discussion and made plans to return the following day to make their final decision. Later that evening, Pee brought his wife to a prestigious restaurant, which was full of important Eurocrats. The same young lady from the bathroom-supply store was working a shift as a waitress. As she passed the Flynns' table, she recognised them and called to Pee in a loud voice, 'Hey! You're the man who needs a shower!'

House proud

When Albert Reynolds first became a minister in 1979, he and his family moved house. One day, one of their former neighbours dropped by. Seeing one of Albert's young daughters out front, he asked, 'So how do you like your new place?'

'It's terrific,' the little girl answered, 'I have my own room and my sisters have their own rooms. But poor Mam is still in with Dad.'

The recognition factor

Fianna Fáil did very badly in the 1992 general election. The next day, party leader Albert Reynolds was a bit nervous as he had to make a public appearance at a major dinner. His nerves were calmed immediately when an old man came to greet him and gave him a big smile and most enthusiastic handshake. 'It's a great, great pleasure to finally meet you in the flesh,' the old man said. 'You are a true icon of the party...what's this your name is again?'

Honesty is the best policy

In 1992, the Irish pound was devalued. In the run-up to the announcement, Albert Reynolds had publicly insisted that no matter what happened Ireland would not devalue. At a press conference two days before the announcement, Albert continued to maintain this public stance. After the press conference, he was approached by a number of journalists who asked him off the record if he was really serious. The word is that Albert took the wind out of their sails by saying: 'Nah, lads. We're f*****.'

The doc

The political establishment was saddened in June 2005 to hear of the death of the former Minister for Justice, Seán Doherty. Seán was one of the 'gang of five' (with Albert Reynolds, Tom McEllistrim, Mark Killilea and Jackie Fahey) who engineered the election of Charles

Haughey as leader of Fianna Fáil in December 1979. Seán's brief career as Minister for Justice in 1982 was synonymous with controversy and intrigue and coincided with the GUBU (Grotesque, Unbelievable, Bizarre, Unprecedented) period. His political career never really recovered from the revelation that he had ordered the bugging of the phones of journalist Geraldine Kennedy and Bruce Arnold. On the *Nighthawks* television programme, Seán claimed for the first time that CJH knew about the wire taps in 1982 and had been given transcripts of the tapes. This helped to bring about the end of Charlie's political career.

There was a lot more to Seán Doherty than met the eye. I first met him in the Basilica in Lourdes pushing a little boy in a wheelchair. He was everything I did not expect him to be from his media image: extremely intelligent and articulate, very witty but also very serious, charming, considerate, kind and, above all, great company. Every subsequent meeting I had with him confirmed this opinion. He was also a wonderful storyteller and many of his stories were told with a mischievous glint in his eye. The following are just a sample.

The Doc's speed of thought was evident at an early age. One day he asked his mother if he could go out and play. She replied, 'What? With those torn trousers?'

Doherty responded quick as a flash, 'No, with the lads down the road.'

The same speed of thought was evident in June 1989, when Seán sensationally lost his seat in the general election. On live television, as he stood in the Roscommon count centre, Brian Farrell asked him: 'Seán Doherty, what went wrong?'

With a typical smile he replied: 'Not enough people voted for me, Brian.'

The Doc lost his seat to the Roscommon Hospital Action Committee candidate, Tom Foxe. Characteristically Doherty promised Foxe, 'You only have the seat on the hire purchase. I will be taking it back in the next election.' True to form, he did.

Fast women

In 1965 Doherty joined the Garda Síochána. While he was a guard, he did a stint catching speeders at a notorious speed trap. One day he saw a car puttering along at 22 miles per hour. He thought to himself, 'That car is just as dangerous as a "speeder".' So he pulled the car over. Approaching the car, he noticed the five old ladies, two in the front and three in the back, wide eyed and as white as ghosts.

The driver obviously confused said, 'Guard, I don't understand, I wasn't doing over the speed limit. What seems to be the problem?' 'Ma'am,' Doherty replied, 'you should know that driving slower than the speed limit can also be dangerous.'

'Slower than the speed limit? No, Sir. I was doing exactly 22 miles an hour,' the old woman said proudly.

Doherty, containing a chuckle, said that N22 was the road number, not the speed limit. A bit embarrassed, the woman grinned, thanking the garda for pointing out her error.

'Before I go Ma'am, I have to ask, is everyone okay? These women seem badly shaken.'

'Oh, they will be alright in a minute, Guard, we just got off the N142.'

Another time, Doherty pulled over a driver for speeding. The man readily admitted his guilt and went on to say, 'It's a good job I wasn't driving a company car. The company I work for frowns on speeding.'

Doherty replied dryly, 'So does the company I work for, Sir.'

An unreliable witness

One of the stories Doherty told about his time as a guard was about the prisoner who accused Doherty of giving him a bloody nose. The Doc explained to the drunk man that he had been so inebriated he had fallen over and hit his head on the pavement. Denying he was drunk, the man claimed that he could produce a witness – a little old lady in a fur coat who had been in the back of the squad car which had escorted him to the garda station. Doherty calmly pointed out that 'the little old lady' was his dog.

Speed

Another time when Doherty was on road duty, he had a problem with an elderly lady. The conversation unfolded as follows:

Elderly lady: 'Is there a problem, Guard?'

Doc: 'Ma'am, you were speeding.'

Elderly lady: 'Oh, I see.'

Doc: 'Can I see your license please?'

Elderly lady: 'I'd give it to you but I don't have one.'

Doc: 'Don't have one?'

Elderly lady: 'Lost it, four years ago for drunk driving.'

Doc: 'I see…Can I see your vehicle registration papers, please?'

Elderly lady: 'I can't do that.'

Doc: 'Why not?'

Elderly lady: 'I stole this car.'

Doc: 'Stole it?'

Elderly lady: 'Yes, and I killed and hacked up the owner.'

Doc: 'You what?'

Elderly lady: 'His body parts are in plastic bags in the boot if you want to see.'

Doherty looked at the woman, slowly backed away to his car and called for back up. Within minutes five garda cars had arrived. A senior guard slowly approached the car, clasping his half-drawn baton.

Guard 2: 'Ma'am, could you step out of your vehicle, please.'

The woman stepped out of her car.

Elderly lady: 'Is there a problem, Guard?'

Guard 2: 'One of my officers told me that you have stolen this car and murdered the owner.'

Elderly lady: 'Murdered the owner?'

Guard 2:'Yes, could you open the boot of your car, please.'

The woman opened the boot, revealing nothing but an empty trunk.

Guard 2:'Is this your car, Ma'am?'

Elderly lady: 'Yes, here are the registration papers.'

Guard 2: 'These are the correct papers.'

The garda was quite stunned.

Guard 2: 'One of my officers claims that you do not have a driving license.'

The woman dug into her handbag and pulled out a license and handed it to the guard. The officer examined the license. He looked quite puzzled.

Garda 2: 'Thank you, Ma'am, one of my officers told me that you didn't have a license, that you stole this car and that you murdered and hacked up the owner.'

Elderly lady: 'Bet the liar told you I was speeding, too.'

Knock, knock

In the 1990s, Doherty rediscovered religion. He could make a joke about it: 'I have appeared in Knock more often than the Virgin Mary!'

In his years as a guard there were clues of his religious sensibilities. Doherty was on traffic duty when he came across a car up on a pavement outside a church. There was a 'No Parking' sign nearby. On the car was a note which read: 'Drove around for 20 minutes, Forgive Us Our Trespasses…' and a £5 note into the bargain. Doherty left the fiver and the note but added a parking ticket and a note of his own. He wrote: 'Been a guard for five years. Lead Us Not Into Temptation.'

The good book

One night, Doherty returned home from evening Mass when he was startled by an intruder. He caught the man in the act of robbing his home of its valuables and yelled, 'Stop! Acts 2:38' (Repent and be baptised, in the name of Jesus Christ so that your sins may be forgiven.)

The burglar stopped in his tracks.

Doherty calmly called the gardaí and explained what he had done.

As the officer handcuffed the man to take him in, he asked the burglar, 'Why did you just stand there? All he had to do was yell scripture at you?'

'Scripture?' replied the burglar. 'He said he had an axe and two 38s!'

A matter of honour

One day, Brian Cowen was approached by an old friend who was down on his luck. The friend asked for a loan of €100. 'I'd like to help you,' said the minister, 'but I can't. I have an arrangement with my bank manager which prevents me from lending you that amount.'

'What do you mean?' asked the friend.

'Well, he promised never to run for the Dáil and I promised never to lend money!'

Outstanding

After his famous 'when in doubt the PDs out' comments, Brian Cowen is reported to have told a story about a conversation between a father and his son.

Father: 'Son, what'll I buy you for your birthday?'

Son: 'A bicycle, please.'

Father: 'What'll I buy you for your First Communion?'

Son: 'A PlayStation?'

Father: 'What'll I buy you for Christmas?'

Son: 'A Mickey Mouse outfit.'

Father: 'No problem, son. I'll just buy you the Progressive Democrats.'

Driving home the point

While he was Minister for Transport, Séamus Brennan gave his daughter a rules of the road book. On the way home to Dundrum one day, he coached her as she drove. He told her to study the rules of the road so that she would be ready when she came to take her driving test.

'Oh,' she said, 'I already know everything in the book.'

'You do?' the Minister returned.

'Yep,' she said, very smugly.

'Okay, we'll just see about that. I'll ask you a hard question. How many feet does it take to stop the car if you are driving 60 miles an hour and have to slam on the brakes really hard?'

'One.'

'What? One?'

She repeated her answer and then because of the confused look on his face, she added: 'Only one, Dad. You always told me only use my right foot on the brake and never my left.'

A dog's life

One night, Séamus Brennan was out canvassing and asked a woman for her vote. She told him to make himself useful. She handed him her dog's lead and told him to take her dog for a walk. He did and got her vote.

Brennan is a Galway man and a keen GAA fan. He pays particular attention to the state of Connacht football. In the run up to the 2005 Connacht championship clash between Sligo and Leitrim, Séamus greatly enjoyed a conversation between Micheál O'Muircheartaigh and Des Cahill on RTÉ radio.

Des: 'How will Leitrim do on Sunday?'

Micheál: 'Leitrim always have hope.'

Des: 'When will we get to a stage when Leitrim have something else besides hope?'

Guess when we're coming to dinner?

When Jim McDaid was a full cabinet minister, he liked to think he had a certain cachet. After a cabinet meeting, the ministers decided to go for a meal in the hottest new restaurant in Dublin. The problem was that everybody else wanted to eat there, so they couldn't get a booking until 10.30 that night. When Jim heard this he was not happy. He convinced his colleagues that he could get an earlier booking, using his position in the cabinet. All the ministers crowded around the telephone to observe Jim's negotiating skills.

'Hello, my friend booked a table with you earlier for 10.30 tonight and I know it's a very busy Saturday night for you but I was wondering if there was any possibility that you could fit us in earlier...My name is Jim McDaid...Yes, that Jim McDaid, the Minister for Fun...Oh no, I couldn't possibly allow you to go to a lot of trouble just for me...Well, the last thing I would want you to think is that because of my status in politics I'm expecting any special treatment…Well, if you absolutely insist it is no trouble to you, that would be fantastic…Fine, fine that's so good of you, I can't thank you enough. You've made all of us very happy. See you soon.'

His cabinet colleagues were awestruck at his apparent influence. However, their admiration quickly dissipated when they asked him what time they would now be eating.

McDaid announced with a flourish: '10.15!'

Strawberries and cream

The former Minister for Agriculture Joe Walsh was driving along the road in his tractor, carrying a load of fertiliser. A child playing in front of his house saw him and called, 'What are you hauling?'

'Fertiliser,' Walsh replied.

'What are you going to do with it?' asked the child.

'Put it on strawberries,' answered Walsh.

'You ought to live in this house,' the child advised him. 'We put sugar and cream on them.'

New direction

After his 'problems' with his PR person early in 2005, Martin Cullen decided to seek public relations advice elsewhere. One of the agencies that pitched for his business explained how they would market the qualifications of famous people:

Julius Caesar: My last job involved a lot of office politics and back stabbing. I'd like to get away from all that.

Jesse James: I can list among my experiences and skills: leadership, extensive travel, logistical organisation, intimate understanding of firearms, and a knowledge of security measures at numerous banks.

Marie Antoinette: My management style has been criticised, but I like to think of myself as a people person.

Joseph Guillotin: I can give your company a head start on the competition.

Hamlet: My position was eliminated in a hostile takeover.

Genghis Kahn: My primary talent is downsizing. In my last job I downsized my staff, my organisation and the population of several countries.

Roadies

A road in Waterford was in a bad condition. Every week as he drove home from Dublin, Martin Cullen had to dodge huge potholes. The day he was appointed Minister for the Environment, Cullen made a call to the relevant authority to get a crew to do something about the road. The next trip he made home he was relieved to see a crew working on the road. On his way back, he noticed that the men were gone but there was no improvement in the road. However, where the crew had been working stood a brand new bright yellow sign with the words 'Rough Road'.

Suffer the little children

Before he became a full-time politician, Minister for the Environment Dick Roche lectured in UCD. During a test he was administering, he noticed that one of his students, who was heavily pregnant, kept rubbing her side. Before she left after class, he asked her, 'Are you okay? I noticed you were holding onto your side.'

'Oh, I'm fine,' she answered. 'It's just that my baby was pushing his foot up and down my ribs, and it hurt a little.'

'Well, that's good,' Roche said, feeling relieved.

'Yeah,' she continued. 'It's strange. He normally sleeps during your class.'

Top of the class

The teachers unions were delighted when Mary Hanafin was appointed Minister for Education because she was a 'real teacher' herself. A real teacher is defined by five characteristics:

1. They grade copies in the car, during television advertisements, in the bathroom and coming up to the Leaving Cert have even been seen grading in Mass.
2. They cheer when they hear that 1 April doesn't fall on a school day.

3. They can't walk past a crowd of kids without straightening up the line.
4. They have disjointed necks from writing on blackboards without turning around.
5. They have to wear strong glasses from trying to read the fine print in teachers' manuals.

Mary is one of the many former teachers who have left their mark on Irish politics. British political commentator Keith Best said, 'Teaching is a good preparation for politics because you have to reply to questions when you don't know the answer.'

Skulduggery

Former Fianna Fáil Senator Des Hanafin was on holiday in the Holy Land and decided to visit the local bazaar. 'Want to buy the genuine skull of Moses?' asked a stall owner.

'Not really,' replied Des. 'It's much too expensive.'

'Well, what about this skull,' said the stall owner, producing another sample. 'This is cheaper because it's smaller. It's the skull of Moses as a child.'

Learning the language

In the wake of the 11 September attacks in the US, Minister for State Joe Jacob went on the Marion Finucane radio programme to reassure the nation. Many people considered it the best piece of unintentional comedy they had ever heard on radio.

After he became a minister, Jacob got an interesting insight into civil servant speak. He heard one of his staff say: 'Where there are visible vapours in ignited carbonaceous material, there is conflagration.' When Jacob asked what this meant, he was told: 'When there's smoke, there's fire.'

Thank you for the music

Government Chief Whip Tom Kitt really enjoyed his man-to-man conversations with his son David, long before David found fame as a singer. There were times when the son verbally beat his father game, set and match.

'Dad, will you help me with my homework?' David asked.

'Sorry, son,' Des replied. 'It wouldn't be right.'

'Well,' David said, 'you could at least try.'

Des had to give out to David after his son had been joking to their neighbours about living in their house. Des shouted at David, 'I don't care if the outside wall is cracked. Stop telling everyone you come from a broken home.'

The other time relations were slightly strained between them was when David had cautiously asked for an increase in his pocket money. Tom tersely told him that this was not on.

'Well, if you can't increase my pocket money, could you give it to me more often?' David replied.

White-collar crime

According to legend, on his first day in prison former Foreign Affairs Minister Ray Burke met his psychotic-looking cell mate. Burke was terrified.

'Don't worry, mate,' said the prisoner when he noticed how scared the former minister looked. 'I'm in for a white-collar crime, too.'

'Oh, really?' said Burke with a sigh of relief.

'Yeah,' said the prisoner. 'I murdered a priest.'

Fame

Before he won a seat in the Dáil in 1997, Jackie Healy-Rea tried to convince his sceptical friend Nick 'the Nixer' that he was one of the best-known people of all time. Jackie brought Nick up to Leinster House and, as soon as they got to the main gate, Nick spotted Bertie Ahern who immediately shouted: 'Howya Jackie? Hope ye're all well in Kerry. Kerry for Sam.'

Jackie winked at Nick. Then he took his friend to the Phoenix Park. As soon as they got to Áras an Uachtarán Mary Robinson came out and waved: 'Good afternoon, Jackie. Would you and your friend like to come in for coffee and a chat?'

As they bade their goodbyes, Jackie turned to his friend and said: 'Now do you believe me that I'm Ireland's most famous man?'

Nick shook his head. 'I'll believe you if you take me to the Vatican and the Pope recognises you.'

So, they flew to Rome. From his papal apartment, Pope John Paul II was giving a blessing to a large audience. When Jackie saw this, he went in and joined the Pope on the balcony. The Pope greeted him effusively and in 16 different languages complimented him on his wonderful cap. Two hours later when he came down from a long chat with the Pope, he was shocked to hear that Nick had been rushed to hospital in an ambulance. Jackie sped to the hospital and discovered Nick lying on a bed in the casualty ward and looking very pale.

'What happened to you?' inquired Jackie.

'I fainted.'

'Why did you faint?'

'Well I was watching you up on the balcony and a fella turned to me and said: "Who's that up there talking to Jackie Healy-Rea?"'

Jim'll fix it

Fianna Fáil's TD for Dublin North and champion of Aer Lingus workers Jim Glennon first came to prominence as an Irish rugby international. Although he is not an arrogant person he does make one proud boast: 'Nobody used his arse better in the line-out than Jim Glennon did!'

When in Brussels...

In the 1980s, a major conference was held in Brussels for leading European politicians. One of the Irish delegates was the Fianna Fáil MEP for Galway, Mark Killilea. Mark's claim to fame is that he once described Fianna Fáil as 'the party that has its dinner in the middle of the day'.

Mark was staying at the hotel in which the conference was being held. He came down for breakfast and sat at a table where three French politicians were tucking into a continental breakfast. As he sat down to eat his more substantial meal, the French politicians said in unison, '*Bon appétite*'. Mark responded by getting up and shaking hands with each of them individually and saying, 'Mark Killilea'. This process was repeated on the next three mornings.

On the Saturday morning Garrett Fitzgerald, who was Taoiseach at the time, was attending his first day of the conference and went down early for breakfast. He was joined at the table shortly after by the three French politicians. As soon as they sat down to begin their meal Garrett said, '*Bon appétite*'. He was astonished when each of the three got up, shook his hand and greeted him with the words 'Mark Killilea'.

Mistaken identity

For some reason, confusion appears to reign at all levels of Fianna Fáil. The British ambassador after an embassy dinner: 'The soup was tepid.'

The former Foreign Affairs Minister Gerry Collins: 'I thought it was chicken!'

Clare and present danger

Gerry Collins was walking on a great estate in Limerick when he stopped to address a solitary fisherman.

'Any luck?' he asked.

'Any luck?' was the answer. 'Why, I got 40 trout out of here yesterday.'

'Do you know who I am?'

'No,' said the fisherman.

'I'm the Minister for Justice and this is a private estate.'

'And do you know who I am?' asked the fisherman quickly.

'No.'

'I'm the biggest liar in Limerick.'

The wee county

Irish politics has always produced interesting characters. Nowhere is this more apparent than in Louth. In the 1980s Louth Fianna Fáiler Frank Godfrey, a keen fowler, attracted the attention of a photographer at the opening of a school by Education Minister Gemma Hussey. Frank shouted, 'When are you going to take a photograph of my cock?'

A Drogheda Urban District Councillor issued one of the most famous quotes in Irish politics: 'Someone has been spreading allegations, and I know who the allegators are.'

Seven Drunken Nights

During his time as a cabinet minister, Bobby Molloy attended Mass every day. One day Molloy approached a drunk who was rolling around the streets of Dublin and said to him, 'I'm glad to see you've turned over a new leaf'.

'Me?' said the drunk in amazement.

'Yes, I was so thrilled to see you at Mass last night.'

'So that's where I was.'

New recruit

At the end of a very long Cumann meeting, former Fianna Fáil Defence Minister Michael Noonan announced that he wished to meet the board in the snug of the local pub. When he got to the pub, Noonan noticed a strange face there.

'You're not a member of the board,' he said.

To which the man in question replied: 'I certainly am. I was at the meeting and I was never more bored in my life!'

Slumber party

The late Fianna Fáil TD Jim Tunney had a penchant for giving long speeches. One dark winter's night he was awoken at 2 am by frantic knocking at his door. As he rubbed the sleep from his eyes he recognised his guest.

'Well, Séamus, what's the problem? Has somebody died?'

'No, Jim.'

'Is somebody sick and needs the last rites?'

'No.'

'Well, why have you woken me up in the middle of an awful night like this?'

'It's like this, Jim. No matter what I do, I can't get my two children to settle down to sleep. I was hoping you would come down to the house and give one of your political speeches. That would put them to sleep very quickly!'

Cavan fever

There is an unfortunate stereotypical image of Cavan people. It is revealed in stories like the one about the Cavan husband who gave his wife lipstick for Christmas every year so that at least he could get half of it back. Nobody has done more to spread this stereotype than the comedian Niall Tobin. Hence the famous question and answer:

Japanese TV presenter: 'The people of Cavan are very generous?'

Niall Tobin: 'They may have that reputation in Japan.'

Former TD and Minister, John Wilson had been a star footballer with Cavan. The story is that when Wilson and the Cavan football team went on a short holiday, the hotel they stayed at put their Gideon Bibles on chains.

Money's too tight to mention

The libel laws forbid me from naming the former Cavan TD who was so mean that, when his 12-year-old son broke his arm playing football, his father tried to get a free X-ray by taking him down to the airport and making him lie down with the luggage.

A fishy story

The late Clare TD Dr Bill Loughnane was a legend in his native Feakle. There were a few Fine Gael supporters, though, who hinted darkly that he 'was fond of a sup'. In an attempt to bridge the political divide, a prominent Fine Gaeler decided to invite Bill for dinner at his family home. All through the meal the Fine Gaeler's son, Pat, kept staring at their guest. He seemed to show particular interest whenever the TD took a drink from his glass of wine. Finally the boy said, 'Mammy, you said that Dr Bill drinks like a fish but he doesn't.'

Just William

'I wish those friends of William's would stop calling him Big Bill,' said the young Bill Loughnane's mother.

'It's only a friendly nickname,' said her husband.

'Yes, but you know how nicknames stick to people. And William hopes to be a doctor.'

Career move

'And why did you leave your last job?' Seán Lemass asked the young applicant for the position of his personal secretary.

'It was something the boss said,' came the reply.

'Was he abusive to you?' asked Lemass in a voice full of concern.

'No, not really.'

'Well then, what did he say?'

'He said: "You're fired".'

The demon drink

A drunk staggered up to Seán Lemass, newspaper in hand, and greeted him politely. Annoyed, Lemass ignored the greeting. However, the drunk was a man on a mission and was not discouraged, 'Excuse me, Sir, but could you tell me what causes arthritis?'

Again Lemass ignored the man. But when the drunk repeated the question, Lemass turned on him impatiently and cried, 'Drinking causes arthritis, that's what! Gambling causes arthritis. Chasing loose women causes arthritis…' And only then, too late, he said, 'Why do you ask?'

To which the drunkard replied, 'Because it says right here in the papers that's what de Valera has!'

Lemass was a staunch believer in an enterprise culture. One of his favourite stories was about Pietro Mascagni. The great Italian composer was getting very irritated by an organ grinder who stood outside his home playing tunes from Mascagni's opera *Cavalleria Rusticana* at about half the correct speed. Mascagni had a grudging admiration for the man for choosing to play tunes from *Rusticana* from all those available. Nonetheless, the composer could stand it no longer and went outside to give the organ grinder a hard time.

'I am Mascagni. Let me show you how to play this music properly so that you will become a successful organ grinder,' Mascagni said, giving the handle of the hurdy-gurdy some vigorous turns.

The following day Mascagni again heard the organ grinder in the street outside and was pleased to hear his tunes being played correctly. Which he looked out, he noticed a sign over the organ which said, 'Pupil of Mascagni'.

Go with the crowd

During an election campaign, a Fianna Fáil TD gave a speech after Sunday Mass in the Pro-Cathedral. His performance was greeted with the frank appraisal of one worshipper: 'That was the worst speech I ever heard. It was complete nonsense.'

The TD, quite disturbed, informed Seán Lemass what the man had said. Lemass replied: 'That poor chap is not really responsible for what he says. He never has an original thought. He just goes around repeating what everybody else is saying!'

Meaty issues

During the Emergency, Seán Lemass went into a butcher's and said, 'I'm returning these sausages as one end is all bread.'

Well, Sir, in these troubled times it's very difficult to make both ends meat.'

The long fellow

Eamonn de Valera had a reputation for being an austere man. One day, he and his wife were walking in the park, when they noticed a young couple lying on the grass and kissing passionately. 'Why don't you do that?' complained Bean de Valera.

'But,' replied Dev, 'I don't even know the woman.'

Dev was a devout Catholic and a regular Mass goer. During Sunday lunch, his wife asked him whether he preferred the sermons of the curate or the parish priest. When he said the curate, he was asked to justify his choice. 'Well, the curate always says "in conclusion" and concludes but the parish priest always says "lastly" and lasts.'

On one of Dev's rare days off, Bean de Valera persuaded her husband to spend the afternoon working in the garden. The physical toil left the great man exhausted. Later that evening one of his children asked him why he was so tired. Dev replied, 'If you think you're too old for growing pains – try digging the garden.'

De Valera had a droll sense of humour. During one cabinet meeting, a cabinet colleague tied himself up in a verbal knot with a series of mixed metaphors. To the confusion of all present, Dev calmly commented: 'To sit on a safety valve is a notoriously dangerous expedient.'

Dev rang Dómhnall O'Buachalla to tell him that the Constitution of 1937 was doing away with his role of Governor General.

Dev spoke apologetically, 'A Dhómhnaill, I have to tell you that you're abolished.'

There was a pregnant pause as the news was digested.

'And I'd like to tell you, a Eamoinn, that you're another!'

During his presidency Eamonn de Valera attended every All-Ireland final – even though by the end of his tenure he was almost totally blind. One of the last All-Irelands Dev attended had a number of controversial refereeing decisions. The losing manager was asked for his thoughts afterwards. He observed: 'Dev saw more of the game than the ref did.'

All creatures great and small

Eamonn de Valera was passing through the West of Ireland and stopped to ask a farmer for the time. 'Just a moment,' said the farmer. He crouched down beside a cow in the pasture and lifted the udder very gently. 'Ten past three,' was the reply.

Dev was astounded, 'How can you tell time just by feeling a cow's udder?'

'Come here and I'll show you,' said the farmer. 'If you crouch down like this and lift up the udder, you can just see the church clock up the hill there.'

Low

Ireland's second president, Seán T. O'Ceallaigh, was a friendly man. However, there was one subject you didn't dare discuss in front of him – his height. Or, should I say, his lack of it.

One day, Seán T. stormed through the door of the Áras and announced angrily, 'Someone just picked my pocket'.

Most of his staff were speechless, except for one who blurted out, 'How could anyone stoop so low?'

Seán T. was the first Irish president to attend a rugby international. The match was being played in October, so the grass was long. As the President was introduced to Irish captain Des O'Brien, he said, 'God bless you, Des. I hope you have a good game.' Then O'Brien heard a booming voice in the crowd, 'Hey, Des, would you ever get the grass cut so we'd bloody well be able to see the President!'

Contractual difficulties

A Fianna Fáil TD was resigning, so the local Cumann decided to present him with a farewell gift. The night of the presentation, the TD had a few glasses too many of porter. As he drove home he crashed his car through a wall, absolutely wrecking his car in the process. A passer-by was soon on hand and recognised the driver, even though the blood was pumping out of his forehead. The politician instructed the passer-by to shine his torch into the car. 'Are you looking for your present?' inquired the Good Samaritan.

'No. I'll find that sometime but I've got a big bottle of whiskey in here somewhere and I want to be certain it didn't break in the crash.'

First impressions

In the 1990s, Fianna Fáil appointed a new General Secretary. The new man felt it was time for a shake up and was determined to rid the party of all slackers. On a tour of Party HQ, the new boss visited the canteen in Mount Street. It was during the regular afternoon tea break, and he noticed a guy leaning against the wall. The room was full of party officials, and the boss wanted to let them know that he meant business!

The new secretary walked up to the guy leaning against the wall and asked, 'How much money do you make a week?'

A little surprised, the young lad looked at him and replied, 'I make £200 a week. Why?'

The secretary handed the guy £1,200 in cash and screamed, 'Here's six weeks' pay, now GET OUT and don't come back.'

Feeling pretty good about himself, the secretary looked around the room and asked, 'Does anyone want to tell me what that tosser did here?'

From across the room came a voice, 'Pizza delivery guy from Domino's.'

Chapter 5 Them and Us

The Civil War was the defining event in Irish politics. One of its enduring legacies is a deep-seated hostility between Ireland's two leading parties, Fianna Fáil and Fine Gael. As this chapter demonstrates, the rivalry has at least the virtue of creating some humorous moments.

Partisan

An old Mayo man, who was a devout Fianna Fáiler, was dying. When it was obvious that he had very little time left, the local priest, a Fine Gaeler, was sent for. After the priest administered the last rites, he asked the old man if he had any last wish. He was astounded when the man asked if he could join the Fine Gael Party. Nonetheless, the priest duly pulled out a membership card for the man and helped him to sign his name for the last time. When the priest left, the man's seven stunned sons crowded around the bed and asked their father why he had made this extraordinary request. With practically his dying breath the old man said: 'Isn't it better for one of them to die than one of our lads.'

Strange but true

In the 1970s, a Fianna Fáil supporter was on his deathbed. With his last breath he gave one final instruction to his family: 'Whatever you do, don't put my death notice in *The Irish Independent*. I don't want any of my hard-earned money going to that Fine Gael paper.'

Riddle me this

Fine Gael supporters tell a number of jokes about their opponents in Fianna Fáil.

Q: What do Fianna Fáilers use for contraception?
A: Their personalities.
Q: How many intelligent Fianna Fáilers does it take to screw a light bulb?
A: Both of them.
Q: What's the difference between God and Charlie Haughey?
A: God doesn't think he's Charlie Haughey.

Drive safely

During the 2005 by-election campaign in Meath, a Fianna Fáil supporter suggested the following to the voters: 'If you support Fianna Fáil, drive with your lights on during the day. If you support Fine Gael, drive with your lights off at night-time.'

Accidental disclosure

A Fianna Fáil supporter and a Fine Gael supporter were in a car accident, and it was a bad one. Both cars (bearing party political stickers) were totally demolished, but amazingly neither of them was hurt.

After they crawled out of their cars, the Fianna Fáiler said, 'So you're a Fine Gaeler, that's interesting. I am a Fianna Fáiler...Wow! Just look at our cars. There's nothing left, but fortunately we are unhurt. This must be a sign from God that we should meet and be friends and live together in peace for the rest of our days.'

The Fine Gaeler replied, 'I agree with you completely; this must be a sign from God!' The Fianna Fáiler exclaimed, 'And look at this – here's another miracle. My car is completely demolished but this bottle of whiskey didn't break. Surely God wants us to drink this and celebrate our good fortune.' Then he handed the bottle to the Fine Gaeler. The Fine Gaeler nodded his head in agreement. He opened the bottle, took a few big swigs and then handed it back to the Fianna Fáiler, who immediately put the cap back on. The Fine Gaeler asked, 'Aren't you having any?'

The Fianna Fáiler replied, 'No. I think I will just wait for the gardaí...'

The gene pool

Shane and Séamus attended a GAA dinner dance in Wicklow during the course of the 2002 general election campaign. They got into an argument about politics. Séamus asked Shane why he was such a dedicated Fine Gaeler. Shane answered that his father and grandfather had both been true blue Fine Gaelers and he was carrying on the family tradition.

'That's it?' said the exasperated Séamus. 'What if your father and grandfather had been horse thieves?'

'Well…' Shane replied, 'I suppose then I'd be a Fianna Fáiler like you.'

Compulsive viewing?

A Fine Gael supporter watching Bertie Ahern on *Prime Time*: 'That was some programme. I'd only have changed one thing.'

His wife: 'What's that?'

'The channel.'

A question of ethos

A man was hitchhiking outside Maynooth. A Mercedes stopped and the driver asked the hitchhiker what his politics were. The man replied, 'I'm a Fine Gaeler.' The driver said, 'I don't allow Fine Gaelers in my car' and drove off. A few minutes later, a BMW stopped and exactly the same thing happened. As soon as the driver found out that the hitchhiker was a Fine Gaeler, he refused to let him into the car. So the man thought, 'Well this is stupid. The next car that stops I'll say that I'm a Fianna Fáiler.'

A couple of minutes later a Porsche stopped. The driver was a stunning blonde. She asked him his politics and he replied that he was a Fianna Fáiler. She told him to get in. He climbed in and noticed that she was wearing a very short miniskirt. As she drove, it climbed further and further up, and he started to get really sexually stimulated. Finally he could stand it no longer, so he turned to her and said, 'You know I've only been a Fianna Fáiler for 10 minutes and already I want to screw somebody!'

Horse sense

A holidaymaker from America found his way into a pub on the Curragh and began some serious drinking. After he was well past the legal limit, he stood up and shouted, 'All Fianna Fáilers are horses asses'.

Immediately, the customers set upon him and beat him to a bloody pulp.

After a few months of healing, the American returned to the same pub and, once again, had more to drink than was reasonable. Staggering to his feet, but remembering what had happened the last time, he shouted, 'All Fine Gaelers are horses asses,' whereupon the crowd descended upon him and beat him to a pulp again.

On his way to the hospital, he complained to the ambulance attendant, 'Who the hell do these people vote for around here?'

'You don't understand,' the attendant replied. 'This is horse country.'

An education

Fianna Fáilers tell the story of three Fine Gaelers who travelled to Dublin by train to attend a match in Croke Park. At the station, the three Fine Gaelers each bought a ticket and watched as a group of Fianna Fáilers only bought a single ticket between three of them. 'How are the three of you going to travel on the train?' asked one of the Fine Gaelers.

'Watch and learn,' replied one of the Fianna Fáilers.

They all boarded the train. The Fine Gaelers took their seats but all three Fianna Fáilers crammed into a toilet and closed the door behind them. Shortly after the train had departed the conductor arrived to collect the tickets. He knocked on the toilet door and said: 'Ticket, please.' The door opened just a crack and a single arm emerged with a ticket in hand. The conductor took it and moved on.

The Fine Gaelers were very impressed, so on the way home after the match they decided to copy their political enemies. When they got to the station, they bought one ticket for the journey. To their amazement, the Fianna Fáilers did not buy a single ticket. 'How are the three of you going to travel on the train?' asked one of the Fine Gaelers.

'Watch and learn,' replied one of the Fianna Fáilers.

Once they boarded, the three Fine Gaelers locked themselves in one toilet, and the three Fianna Fáilers locked themselves into another one nearby. The train departed. A short while afterwards, one of the Fianna Fáilers left the toilet and knocked on the toilet door where the Fine Gaelers were locked in. 'Ticket, please,' he said.

Puzzling

Especially since Martin Cullen's much-reported troubles with electronic voting, Fine Gael politicians love to belittle Cullen's intellectual capabilities. Michael Noonan's joke is particularly popular. One morning, Cullen rang the Taoiseach and sounding rather upset, he mumbled, 'Bertie, I don't think I'll be at the cabinet meeting this morning. I am having trouble with this jigsaw puzzle and I'm not going anywhere until I have solved it.'

Bertie replied, 'Well, what sort of jigsaw puzzle is it?'

Cullen said, 'It's got a picture of a tiger on the box but none of the pieces seem to fit together.'

Bertie, rather annoyed by now, said, 'Okay, give me five minutes and I'll come over and see what I can do.'

After a while, Bertie reached Cullen's office and was greeted by Cullen's media advisor. She took Bertie into the office where Cullen was sitting at the table, shuffling the orange pieces and looking confused.

Bertie looked at him, immediately realised what had happened and said, 'Martin, for God's sake put the Frosties back in the box!'

After the media furore about the awarding of state contracts, Enda Kenny got in on the act and told a joke about Cullen. Kenny told the tale of Cullen, Albert Einstein and Séamus Heaney going to heaven. When they got to the gate, St Peter was introducing an identity check. He began with Einstein who proved his identity by demonstrating the theory of relativity. Einstein was then welcomed into heaven. Next Séamus Heaney proved himself by composing an incredible poem about the gates of heaven. Heaney was warmly welcomed into heaven. Then St Peter turned to Cullen and said: 'Albert Einstein and Séamus Heaney have demonstrated their identity very decisively. How are we to know that you are who you say you are?'

A blank look came over Cullen's face and after a few minutes of thought he asked: 'Who are Albert Einstein and Séamus Heaney?'

St Peter beamed a beatific smile and said: 'Well answered. You really are Martin Cullen. Make yourself at home here in heaven.'

Doomed

Last December, a particularly acrimonious debate took place in the Dáil between the government and the opposition. With the season of goodwill approaching, Bertie Ahern, Enda Kenny, Pat Rabbitte, Mary Harney and Trevor Sargent held a crisis meeting to try to restore harmony. Eventually, they decided to produce a cross-party Nativity play. Sadly the plans had to be quickly scrapped. They couldn't find anybody to play the three wise men.

Chapter 6 Garrett the Good

Watching Garrett is habit forming,
It can become habitual,
It's a kind of long-lasting political ritual.
Since his retirement it may not be the number one prerogative,
but to ignore him is only for the slogative.

In 1982, under the leadership of Garrett Fitzgerald, Fine Gael came close to replacing Fianna Fáil as Ireland's largest party. Politics in Ireland in the 1980s was dominated by the battle between Charlie Haughey and 'Garrett the Good'. Garrett was a formidable intellect; had a great love of statistics, talked very quickly and sometimes wore odd shoes. Stories about him abound.

No rugger bugger

Garrett was a pupil of the Jesuits in Belvedere, and there was exposed to a different kind of religion – rugby. The romance did not last very long as Garrett recognised in his adult years, 'I played rugby once. Then I discovered that you had to run with the ball so I gave it up.'

And so this is Christmas

In 1973, Garrett became Minister for Foreign Affairs. He was a big hit with journalists everywhere, but especially with BBC journalists, who rejoiced in his towering intellectual gifts. At the start of December that year, the head of news at the BBC rang Garrett to thank him for all his help during the year. Then the BBC rep asked Garrett what he wanted for Christmas. With his high ethical standards, Garrett said that he didn't think it was a very good idea. However, the BBC rep insisted, and in the end Garrett said he wanted a small box of chocolates. The BBC rep seemed a little puzzled at this answer, but they ended the conversation and Garrett thought nothing more of it.

Later that month, on Christmas Eve, Garrett was sitting watching the BBC news on TV with his wife, Joan. An item came on about what leading politicians wanted for Christmas. It was reported in a matter-of-fact way that 'the British Prime Minister wanted world peace; the President of the United States stated that he wanted a cure for cancer and the Irish Foreign Minister said that he wanted a small box of chocolates'.

The ambassador's ball

At an ambassador's banquet in 1976, one of the lady guests complained a bit too loudly that, according to the official order of preference, she ought to be seated next to the Minister for Foreign Affairs. Feeling somewhat embarrassed at the fuss she had made, the lady said to Garrett Fitzgerald: 'You must find these questions of precedence extremely troublesome.'

'Not really,' was the reply. 'We have found by experience that the people who matter don't mind, and that people who mind don't matter.'

For better or worse

Garrett always said that his wife Joan was central to his life. One of the stories told about their relationship was that from their wedding day, their friends knew what the Fitzgerald's marriage would be like. The priest asked Joan: 'Do you take this man to be your husband?'

And she said, 'I do.'

Then the priest asked Garrett, 'Do you take this woman to be your wife?' and Joan replied, 'He does'.

A red scare

Garrett was not known for his interest in hurling. His lack of hurling knowledge was most graphically illustrated on a trip to Cork. Garrett became Taoiseach in 1981, at a time of national crisis. The economy was in tatters and the IRA's hunger strike policy was at its height in the North. One of the few good news stories at this time was the rise of Solidarity, the trade union movement in Poland. Many believed that this would eventually lead to the collapse of Communism. The fact that everybody knew that Pope John Paul II, who had visited Ireland two years earlier, was involved in Solidarity added to the interest in the story. Most people in Ireland knew that the Solidarity colours were red.

Garrett arrived in Cork on a Sunday and saw hordes of people swathed in red and white. The Taoiseach did not realise that these people were on their way to a Munster Championship match. Very impressed at such a display of political activism, Garrett is said to have turned to his aide and remarked, 'I never knew Solidarity had such popular support in Cork.'

On the canvas trail in 1981, Garrett posed for a photo opportunity swinging a hurl. He allegedly said to a journalist, 'I've always wanted to play hurling so I thought it would be a good thing to learn the rudiments of the game.'

His interviewer asked, 'So have you learned much?'

Garrett replied, 'Yes, I have. How to swing a cue.'

Offaly smart

During one of the two general elections in 1982, Garrett gave a speech in Birr, Co. Offaly, about the need to help the poor in the developing world. Not surprisingly Garrett brought statistics into his speech. Sensing that he may have started speaking over the head of his audience, he tried to illustrate his point by using examples. He posed a rhetorical question, 'Do you realise that every time I breathe someone dies?'

A heckler shouted up, 'Did you ever try sucking mints?'

Mr Chips

One night, a Fine Gael cabinet meeting ran so late that a secretary was sent out to buy fish and chips. Ever worried about protocol, Garrett considered it undignified for the Taoiseach to eat out of a paper bag, so he poured his chips into a crystal bowl in the centre of the table. Little did he know, Alan Dukes had been using it as an ashtray for the previous six hours. Collective responsibility took on a new dimension as everyone gave a few chips to the Taoiseach.

Technological advance
Japanese scientists have created a camera with such a fast shutter speed that they can now photograph Garrett with his mouth shut.

The national handlers
At one stage, Garrett's handlers decided that he needed to become more aware of pop culture. They had explained to Taoiseach that Yoko Ono was a singer (using the term in its broadest sense). He had thought it was Japanese for 'one egg please'.

They call me Garth
American country star Garth Brooks was hugely popular in Ireland – at least until Ronan Keating covered his song 'If Tomorrow Never Comes'. After playing Croke Park, Garth found himself in the company of Garrett Fitzgerald and they had an erudite conversation. Garth's former wife, Sandy, asked the singer what they had talked about.

'We talked about philosophy. He had no difficulty proving to me that I don't exist.'

Identity crisis
During the 1987 general election, Garrett Fitzgerald visited a home for the elderly which offered specialist care to those suffering from senile dementia. After the initial introductions, Garrett settled down to speak to individual residents. He made polite conversation with a reserved looking woman. After it became clear that the woman didn't really understand what was happening, Garrett gently asked: 'Do you know who I am?'

The woman sadly shook her head and replied: 'No, but if you go and ask matron, she'll tell you. She knows everyone in here.'

For whom the bell tolls

After dinner one evening, Garrett went for a walk though Ranelagh. On Sandford Road, he noticed a little boy frantically trying to reach a doorbell. Being a kind man, Garrett took pity on the child and lifted him up to ring the bell. When the bell rang, Garrett said: 'Now what?'

The little boy replied: 'Now, we run.'

Chapter 7 The Blueshirts

Fine Gael has long been – to use the language of political correspondents – 'no stranger to controversy'. Historically, it has been portrayed as the party of big farmers. Although the popular perception is that Fine Gaelers are a dull bunch, they have generated more fun than many people might have expected.

The letter

In 1996, a little boy in Roscommon wanted £100 very badly and his mother told him to pray to God for it. He prayed and prayed for two weeks, but nothing turned up. Then he decided perhaps he should write God a letter requesting the £100.

When the post sorters at An Post received the letter addressed to God, they opened it and forwarded it to the Taoiseach, John Bruton. John was so impressed, touched and amused that he instructed his secretary to send the boy a cheque for £5. He thought this would be a lot of money to a little boy.

The little boy was delighted with the £5 and sat down to write a thank you letter to God, which ran as follows:

Dear God,

Thank you very much for money. I noticed that you had to send it through the government. As usual, they deducted £95 for themselves.

Liam

Customer relations

In his bachelor days, John Bruton was known to occasionally frequent fast food restaurants. Once he went to McDonald's and said, 'I'd like some fries'. The girl at the counter asked, 'Would you like some fries with that?'

Slim pickings

A few years ago, John Bruton went to his doctor, who suggested that John's health might improve if he lost a few pounds. The doctor said: 'This is the diet you must follow. Three lettuce leaves, a slice of dry toast and a glass of orange juice twice a day.'

Bruton replied, 'I see. Now is that before meals or after?'

Skin care

In 1995, John Bruton went into the barber's shop and asked for a shave. The barber was fond of a drink and struggling with a hangover. His hands were shaking. Soon the Taoiseach's face was covered in tiny, little cuts. Exasperated, he said to the barber: 'The drink is an awful thing, Séamus.'

The barber took a second before replying: 'You're right about that, Mr Bruton. 'Tis awful. Sure the drink, Mr Bruton…it makes the skin awful soft.'

The patter of tiny feet

Three months after Enda Kenny got married, his wife said to him, 'I have great news for you. Pretty soon, there is going to be three in this house instead of two.'

Enda, glowing with happiness, kissed his wife and said: 'Oh darling, I'm the happiest man in the world.'

Then she said, 'I'm glad that you feel this way, because tomorrow morning my mother moves in with us.'

An unexpected response

Enda Kenny was driving from Mayo to Dáil Eireann. He got stuck at traffic lights behind a car with a bumper sticker that said, 'Honk if you love Jesus.'

So he honked. The driver leaned out his window, gave him a very impolite gesture, and yelled, 'Can't you see the light is still red, you moron?'

Ah, ref

Enda Kenny once volunteered to referee a charity football match. His friend came with him to watch. On the sideline, a father behind Enda's friend boasted, 'That's my son!' The boy, who had been playing so well up to that point, then proceeded to miss four open goals.

'Well,' came the voice behind him, 'maybe not. They all look alike from over here.'

After the game was over, Enda asked his friend if he thought he had been fair to both teams.

'Yes,' he replied thoughtfully. 'Both teams hated you about the same.'

Movie news

Without realising it, Enda Kenny walked right into a garda stakeout at his local Xtravision. When a young man stepped out the door, two guards pounced, cuffing him and hustling him into a squad car.

Seeing the manager's astonished expression, Enda said: 'When you guys say the movie is due by noon the next day...you really mean it.'

High energy

As education spokesperson for Fine Gael, Olwyn Enright once visited the Young Scientist Exhibition. She prepared for the visit by reading up on science matters. She asked one of the participants: 'What is the relationship between kinetic and potential energy?'

At first the student looked stumped, but he rallied and replied, 'As far as I know, they're just friends, but there could be something else going on there.'

Zero tolerance

In 1983, a man got a job as a night watchman in the Department of Justice. There had been a lot of thefts, so every morning when the night shift workers passed through his gate the man had to check their bags and pockets to make sure that nothing was being stolen.

The first night on the job, things were going along very well until a man came through his gate pushing a wheelbarrow of newspapers. 'Aha,' the night watchman thought, 'that man thinks he can cover up what he is stealing with them newspapers.' So he removed the papers and found nothing.

Still he felt that the man was acting strangely, so he questioned him about the paper. 'I get a little extra money from newspapers I recycle, so I go into the lunchroom and pick up all the ones people have thrown away.' The guard let him pass, but decided to keep a close eye on him.

The next night was the same, and the night after that. Week after week it went on. The same guy pushed the wheelbarrow of newspapers past the guard's checkpoint. The guard always checked and found nothing.

Then one night, about a year later, the guard reported for work to find a message telling him to report to the Minister for Justice, Michael Noonan. He walked into the minister's office, and before he could say a word, Noonan roared, 'You're fired'.

'Fired?' he asked in total surprise. 'Why? What did I do?'

'It was your job to make sure that no one stole anything from this Department and you've failed. So you're fired'.

'Hang on a second, what do you mean failed? Nobody ever stole anything from this place while I was on guard.'

'Oh, really,' Michael Noonan answered. 'Then how do you account for the fact that there are 365 wheelbarrows missing?'

An age-old problem

Many were scornful of Michael Noonan's claims that Fine Gael would do well in the 2002 general election. To illustrate they told the story of a crocodile-infested river in Africa. On the other side of the river, there was a tribe which various missionaries wanted to convert. However, nobody was willing to take the risk of crossing the river. In spring 2002, along came a group of missionaries who waded across the river without coming to any harm. Shortly after they revealed their secret. 'We wore T-shirts bearing the words Fine Gael, general election winners, 2002. And sure not even a crocodile was willing to swallow that!'

Dukes of Hazard

In 1982, Garrett Fitzgerald made Alan Dukes Minister for Finance. One of the many controversies that sprung up around Dukes at the time had nothing to do with politics. Switzer's ran a short-lived ad for in-store credit cards which carried the slogan, 'It's time he gave you one, Mrs Dukes'.

In 1987, Dukes succeeded Garrett as leader of Fine Gael. Not all Fine Gael TDs were impressed. The following year, Galway TD John Donnellan was expelled from the parliamentary party for his comment about Dukes, 'If it was raining soup, he'd have a fork in his hand'.

Band of brothers

Another opponent of Dukes within the party was the late Jim Mitchell. Michael McDowell described Jim as, 'the evil of two lessers' – at a stroke striking a second blow against Jim's brother, Gay.

Jim Mitchell once complained to an Ceann Comhairle, Joe Brennan: 'You're always mixing me up with someone else.'

Brennan replied, 'Yes, I'm always confusing you with that fellow Mitchell.'

O, Gay

In a previous incarnation, Fine Gael MEP for Dublin Gay Mitchell produced a number of quiz books. Down the years, they have provided much entertainment in the Dáil bar, largely because of the wrong answers they have elicited. A sample is included below:
Mitchell: 'With what town in Britain is Shakespeare associated?'
TD: 'Hamlet'
Mitchell: 'Name the BBC's Grand Prix Commentator? I'll give you a clue, it's something you suck.'
TD: 'Oh, Dickie Davies!'

Mitchell: 'What is Chris Lloyd's maiden name?'
TD: 'Chris de Burgh'

Identity test

A man in great distress arrived in the constituency clinic of Olivia Mitchell. He had just been assaulted.

'Can you describe your assailant?' Olivia asked as she handed the man a cup of tea.

'Of course I can! That's what I was doing when he hit me.'

Are you wrong there, Michael?

Michael Lowry had a huge impact on Fine Gael's reputation, after it was revealed that Ben Dunne had financed the renovations of the TD's home. Mary Harney said, 'To date in 1996, we [the PDs] have received £35,000 in corporate donations. That wouldn't be enough to build a conservatory onto Deputy Lowry's house.'

Sheepish

When Gemma Hussey was Minister for Education, she visited a rural school in Wicklow. She joined the class during religious instruction. The teacher talked to the pupils about the stories in the Bible. He introduced the story of the Good Shepherd. 'Now boys and girls,' he asked, 'who would you expect to find in the middle of a flock of sheep?' A young boy put up his hand and replied, 'A ram, Sir.'

Nun sense

Sr Rita, a teacher, was a legendary figure in Galway. She was a singularly impatient woman who never took no for an answer. When a serious problem arose in her school in the mid-1970s, caused by some new directive from the Department of Education, she went straight to Minister Dick Burke's office to get an exemption for her school. Sr Rita was blocked by the minister's attractive blonde receptionist. The nun said, in a tone that defied contradiction, 'Now look here, Missie, you are here for your looks not your brains. Don't you tell me what I can or cannot do. After all I am doing God's work; you are only doing the minister's.'

Lovely Leitrim

On Sunday 24 July, 1994, Leitrim's luck finally turned. The county ended 67 years in the wilderness to beat Mayo in the Connacht final by 0–12 to 2–4. Some people credited the win to their coach John O'Mahony, but others argued divine intervention was responsible. On the morning of the match, the former Fine Gael TD for Leitrim Gerry Reynolds said, 'Leitrim for Croke Park. Mayo for Croagh Patrick.'

Kelly's anti-heroes

The late John Kelly, a former Fine Gael minister, was one of the wittiest people ever to enter Irish politics. In 1979, Ireland suffered a spate of strikes. One of the longest and most disruptive involved An Post workers, which meant nobody in Ireland got letters for weeks. Most people were irate about the government's apparent unwillingness to bring the strike to an end.

The strike coincided with the Fine Gael Ard Fheis. During his speech, John Kelly recalled an imaginary conversation between two members of the Politburo in Communist Russia. One was outraged that a new Department of Private Enterprise had been created in Russia, even though there was no private enterprise allowed in the state. He claimed that such a department was pointless and a drain on resources. His colleague tried to console him, 'Comrade, relax. It is common practice throughout the world to create ministries that are completely useless. Look at decadent America. They have a Minister for Culture – even though you and I know they have no culture. In Switzerland they have a Minister for the Navy, even though the country is completely landlocked. And of course think of the Irish.'

'What about the Irish?'

'Well, they have a Minister for Posts and Telegraphs.'

Labourers in the vineyard

Reporter: 'How many people work in the Dáil?'
John Kelly: 'Oh, about half of them.'

The whole caboodle

John B. Keane was one of Kerry's favourite sons. John B. was a prominent Fine Gael supporter. During one particularly vicious general election campaign, John B. decided to inject laughter and reduce the bitterness. So he put up a mock candidate, who went by the name of Tom Doodle. Doodle was the pseudonym given to a local labourer. His slogan, depicted on posters all over the town, was: 'Vote the Noodle and Give the Whole Caboodle to Doodle.'

John B. had organised a brass band and a large crowd to accompany the candidate at his election meeting. Doodle travelled to the town square standing on the back of a donkey-drawn cart. It was a tumultuous affair. In a speech that poked fun at the clientelist, promise-all politics of the time, Doodle declared his fundamental principle: 'Every man should have more than the next.'

Thy kingdom come

Kerry are the undisputed kings of Gaelic football. In the glory days of the 1970s, Jimmy Deenihan was one of the stars of the greatest Kerry teams of them all. A bad injury caused Deenihan to retire prematurely, but he went on to forge a new career in politics. Entering politics was a bit of a culture shock for him, particularly as he got some weird requests from his constituents. The most strange was from the woman who asked him to see if he could arrange 'infidelity benefit' for herself and her husband.

Deenihan's passion for Gaelic football is as strong today as it was in his playing days. His wife saw this at first hand while watching him filling in a credit card application form. When it came to the question that asked: 'What is your position in the company?' He answered: 'Right full-back'.

Right and wrong

The former Fine Gael Taoiseach Liam Cosgrave was the strong, silent type. Asked in 1975 to explain why he was so reticent with the media after a budget, Cosgrave replied: 'It takes a big man to admit when he's wrong, but an even bigger one to keep his mouth shut when he's right.'

During his time as Taoiseach between 1973 and 1977, Cosgrave did not give many interviews. He was very phlegmatic and appeared to live by the wise words of David Brent, star of *The Office:* 'Accept that some days you are the pigeon, and some days you are the statue.'

One day a journalist called to his home seeking an interview. He asked Liam's daughter if her father was at home.

'No,' said the girl.

'Are you sure? I thought I heard his voice.'

The girl turned and shouted into the house, 'Daddy, he's calling me a liar!'

Cosgrave was very keen on spreading his faith. At the height of the conflict in the Middle East he said, 'I appeal to them [the Jews and the Muslims] to settle their differences in accordance with Christian principles.'

A drop of the creatur

In 1957, former judge Patrick J. Lindsay was elected for Fine Gael in Mayo-North. He once went on holiday in west Galway and went into an old pub in a remote area for a pint. 'Did you ever try a drop of poteen?' asked the friendly proprietor. 'No,' said the judge, 'but I have tried a few men who did.'

Tight fist

After a tense debate in the Dáil between W.T. Cosgrave and Eamonn de Valera, Cosgrave said of his opponent: 'He's so mean that if he owned the Atlantic Ocean he wouldn't give you a wave.'

Sickness and health

When she contested the presidential election in 1997, Mary Banotti became one of the best-known faces in Irish politics. As a grand-niece of Michael Collins and as a sister of the former Minister for Justice, Nora Owen, Mary's ascent to the top of the political ladder was, perhaps, not that surprising. In 1982, totally out of the blue, she received one of the biggest shocks of her life when she was diagnosed with diabetes. One of her friends presented her with a large notice to hang around her neck. It read, 'I am a highly intelligent, newly diagnosed diabetic. In the event of any problem, only a bishop will do!'

At the table of the Lord

Michael Collins was a trainee altar boy serving Mass. During the offertory, the priest emptied the cruet of wine into the chalice, to the shock of the trainee. When he came home his mother asked how he had got on at Mass. 'All right,' he said, 'But you know that priest? The way he uses wine, it's a barman he needs, not an altar boy.'

Once bitten twice shy

Michael Collins was known for his generosity. One morning, he returned home from a trip with such a tiny amount of change in his pocket that he gave his last penny to the hotel porter. However, he soon forgot this. When he was approached by a tramp at the bus station, with characteristic generosity, he invited the down-and-out to dine with him for breakfast in the local restaurant.

After a slap-up meal, Collins went to pay the bill, only to discover there was nothing in his pocket. The tramp, seeing his predicament, paid for both of them.

Mortified, Collins said: 'Come with me in a taxi to my home and I will pay you back.'

'No way,' replied the tramp. 'You've caught me for a meal, but there's no way you're getting a taxi fare out of me as well.'

Chapter 8 In Labour

Politics is liberally sprinkled with boot-room banter, boardroom battles, thrilling tricksters and walls of waffle. The Labour Party is Ireland's second oldest party. In its long history, it has provided Irish politics with a motley crew of interesting individuals, who have created some moments of mischief, mirth and mayhem. This chapter pays homage to some of the more memorable characters and plots a humorous and sometimes acerbic course through the third force in Irish politics.

Forgive us our trespasses

Dick Spring enjoyed a close personal relationship with Fergus Finlay. Fergus had unexpectedly forgotten his friend's birthday and sat down to write a letter of apology. It read as follows: 'Dear Dick, I beg your forgiveness for forgetting your birthday and it would serve me right if you forgot my birthday next Friday.'

Deep throat

A woman in Kerry bumped into her next-door neighbour, the wife of Dick Spring, and asked: 'How's your husband?'

'He's laid up in bed with a rugby injury.'

'I didn't know he played.'

'He doesn't any more. He sprained his larynx at the match last Sunday.'

Labour of love

Dick Spring has an impressive sporting and political pedigree. In 1940, his father, Dan Spring, of Kerins O'Rahilly's, captained Kerry to All-Ireland football victory. Three years later, Dan was elected Labour TD for Kerry North, a seat he held until 1981. He was also parliamentary secretary to the Minister for Local Government between 1956 and 1957. Dick jokes, 'In Kerry we have taken and applied the words of the Olympic motto "Higher, Faster, Stronger" for our sporting heroes. As has been said of the Jesuits: "We are tops in everything, including modesty." But modesty is not something Kerry people have had much opportunity to experience. I still follow the progress of club football in Kerry, including teams like Laune Rangers. Someone said that once Tonto became their manager, they became the best side in Kerry. This reminds me of the Galway wit who described an old Corinthians team as being the best since St Paul wrote to them!'

In 1979, Spring won three rugby caps for Ireland. The most remembered incident in his rugby career came against Wales. Spring missed a catch that cost Ireland a crucial try in its 24–21 defeat. While his political career flourished, Spring has never been allowed to forget that episode and has been the butt of jokes about 'a safe pair of hands'. On the enormously popular RTÉ Radio One series *Scrap Saturday*, Spring was consistently referred to as 'Butterfingers'.

Spring used his rugby career to his political advantage: 'Occasionally it came in handy when I was giving speeches. Sometimes when I wanted to get an audience's attention I said Fergus Slattery, Tom Kiernan, Willie John McBride and myself have 153 international caps between us. I didn't mention that I only got three of them! I used another trick when I gave a speech to a rugby audience in Wales. To get their attention, I spoke in Irish for the first three minutes. By the time I started speaking in English they were ready to hang on to my every word!'

'John Major was quite impressed when he heard I played for Ireland. He played rugby himself when he was very young but didn't prosper at the game. John's great passion is cricket and his moods fluctuated a lot depending on the fate of the English team. I was always wary about having sensitive negotiations about the peace process with John when England was playing. The best time to negotiate with him was when England was doing very well – mind you that didn't happen very often!'

74

A good walk shared

Dick Spring is a passionate golfer and, unlike his one-time partner on the fairways, Bill Clinton, a talented one. Dick's love for the game was particularly evident when he joined his wife during her pregnancy classes. The instructor was teaching the women how to breathe properly, along with informing the men how to give the necessary assurances. The teacher then announced, 'Ladies, exercise is good for you. Walking is especially beneficial. And, gentlemen, it wouldn't hurt you to take the time to go walking with your partner.'

The room fell really quiet. Finally, Dick raised his hand. 'Yes?' replied the teacher.

'Is it all right if she carries a golf bag while we walk?'

Honesty is not always the best policy

Dick Spring was once asked what his golf handicap was. He replied, 'Honesty'.

Keeping it in the family

When Spring led Labour into coalition government with Fianna Fáil, Niamh Breathnach was made a minister. She appointed her daughters to a job in the department. One wag suggested that it gave a whole new angle to the 'mother and child' scheme.

The man from Clare

In the 1992 general election Moosajee Bhamjee was elected Labour Party TD for the Clare constituency. Moosajee did a charity parachute jump in aid of the training fund for the Clare hurling team. Before he jumped from the plane, he was told that, as he fell, he should pull the string on his right. In the unlikely event of that not working, he should pull the string on his left. In the highly unlikely event of neither working, he should pray to Mohammed.

The Clare TD jumped, but nothing happened when he pulled the string on his right. So he pulled the string on his left. Again nothing happened. He frantically said a prayer to Mohammed. Immediately a hand came down from heaven and grabbed hold of him. The relieved

Clare TD said with feeling: 'Thank God.' Immediately the hand released him and he was sent hurtling to the ground.

Long-winded

Proinsias de Rossa rose to the top of the political tree, despite the apparent handicap of a speech impediment. He says, 'I'm told that Moses had a stammer. I use the joke that if he hadn't had a stammer, we'd only have two commandments because he was forced to use a lot of word substitution!'

Michael D.

Michael D. Higgins is one of the few TDs who have been immortalised in song. Tuam's most famous sons, the Saw Doctors, celebrated the politician's many talents in the 'classic', 'We've got Michael D. rocking in the Dáil'.

Michael D. championed the cause of civil rights in Central America, long before it was fashionable or profitable. In the early 1980s, the Labour Party was tearing itself apart with internal wrangling about its stance on entering coalition government. An important meeting was called to try to resolve the turmoil. Michael D. was due to speak at it, but at the last moment he cancelled because he had to fly to El Salvador. Frank Cluskey remarked: 'Given the choice between saving the world and saving the Labour Party, Michael D. chose the easy option and decided to save the world.'

Arty

Having been appointed Minister for Arts, Culture and the Gaeltacht and having established a reputation as a poet, Michael D. Higgins decided he should try his hand as an artist. He went to an art supply shop. The shop sold artists' canvas by the yard, in two widths, 36 inches or 48 inches.

Michael D. asked: 'Can you please cut some canvas for me?'

The assistant replied: 'Certainly, what width?'

Michael D. (confused and slightly annoyed): 'Scissors?'

Michael D. has been credited with establishing the Irish film industry on an international plane. His ministerial job brought him face to face with many celebrities. According to one of the stories, Michael D. met the *Baywatch* star David Hasslehoff, who informed the minister that he wanted to be called simply, 'Hoff'.

Michael D. coolly replied: 'No hassle.'

Prince of thieves

Michael D. Higgins: 'Can I have a violin string, please?'
Shop assistant: 'Do you want a steel one?'
Michael D.: 'No, I want to buy one.'

Rough Justice

A farmer and a butcher were engaged in a legal action over a plot of land. The case was listed for the Christmas session. Michael O'Leary, a former Labour leader who later became a Fine Gael TD, was the lawyer engaged by the farmer. O'Leary told his client: 'I'm afraid we have no hope of winning the case.'

The farmer asked: 'Supposing if, as it's Christmas time, I sent a nice turkey with my name on it to the judge, would that help?'

'That would ruin our chances completely,' said O'Leary.

When the case was heard the judge found in favour of the farmer. 'I can't understand how we won,' said O'Leary.

'It must be the turkey I sent to him.'

'You did?' gasped O'Leary.

The farmer answered: 'I did but I put the other fellow's name on it.'

Ordinary decent criminal

Prisoner: 'I used to make big money...'
Former leader of the Labour Party, Frank Cluskey on a trip to Mountjoy: 'How big?'
Prisoner: 'About a quarter of an inch too big.'

Unfit for publication

The former Labour leader Brendan Corish went to Enniscorthy to address a gathering. He began by requesting reporters not to publish any of his speech, as he would be giving the same talk the following week in a neighbouring town. The following day, he was horrified to read in the local paper: 'Mr Corish delivered an excellent talk – he told some wonderful stories – unfortunately they cannot be printed.'

Here's to you, Mrs Robinson

When Mary Robinson was President, she visited a school in her native Mayo. She was questioning a First Communion class on religion. She decided to begin with an easy question and said to the little boy at the front, 'Now, Jack, can you tell me where God lives?'

'I can, Mrs President,' the boy answered. 'He lives upstairs in Murphy's pub.'

The President was very puzzled by this and asked him why he thought that.

'Well, Mrs President, when I was coming into school this morning, the Boozer Jones was standing looking up at the top windows of Murphy's pub and shouting, "Good God, are you not up yet?"'

Weighty matters

As a medical doctor, Noel Browne was concerned about the health of very overweight people. He once dropped a subtle hint to a Labour party colleague. Browne told him about an overweight man on a crowded bus, who said to a schoolboy, 'Why don't you be a gentleman and give a lady your seat?'

The schoolboy replied, 'Why don't you be a gentleman and give two ladies your seat?'

A patient came into Browne's surgery and said, 'Doctor, I can't understand why I'm suddenly putting on weight'.

The doctor replied, 'It's a question of age. Middle age is when the broad mind and narrow waist change places.'

Browne also disliked seeing patients drink too much. He once attempted to reform a patient by asking and answering his own question:

'In which month do the Irish drink the least Guinness?'

'February.'

Medical experimentation

One of Browne's patients was only 30 but was a bit of a wreck. The concerned doctor told him to give up smoking, drinking, eating rich food and chasing women. 'Will that help me to live longer?' asked the patient.

'Hopefully,' said the doctor, 'but I'm not sure. You see no one has tried it yet.'

Blowing his own trumpet

A patient said to Noel Browne, 'And when my right arm is quite better, will I be able to play the trumpet?'

The doctor replied, 'Most certainly – you should be able to play it with ease.'

'That's wonderful – I could never play it before.'

Dead cert

'Are you sure,' an anxious patient asked Noel Browne, 'that I'll recover? I've learned that doctors sometimes give wrong diagnoses and treat patients for kidney problems who later die of something else.'

'That's nonsense,' said Browne. 'If I treat a patient for kidney problems, he dies of kidney problems.'

Designer genes

A married couple had jet-black hair, so when their daughter was born a redhead, the husband was a bit suspicious. He went to Noel Browne and explained the situation.

The doctor asked, 'Well, how often do you have sex?'

'Oh, about once every two years,' replied the husband.

'Well, that explains it,' said the doctor. 'You're a bit rusty.'

Selective memory

A female patient came into Browne and said, 'I get terrible headaches, black outs and dizzy spells and I find it hard to concentrate.'

The doctor inquired, 'What age are you, Madam?'

'Only 30.'

Browne raised his eyebrows, 'So your memory is affected too?'

Father of the pride

Noel Browne was on holiday in a remote part of the West of Ireland. As there was no doctor in attendance locally, he got a call when a farmer's wife went into labour. The farmer's house had no running water, no electricity, none of the creature comforts. The anxious husband, Paddy Joe, asked: 'What d'ya want me to do, Doctor?'

'Hold the lantern, Paddy Joe. Here it comes.' The doctor delivered the child and held it up for the proud father to see, 'Paddy Joe, you're the proud father of a fine strapping boy.'

'Saints be praised, I…'

Before Paddy Joe could finish, Noel Browne interrupted, 'Wait a minute. Hold the lantern.' Soon Dr Browne delivered the next child, 'You've a full set now, Paddy Joe. A beautiful baby daughter.'

'Thanks be to…'

Again Browne cut in, 'Hold the lantern, Paddy Joe. Hold the lantern.' Soon the doctor delivered a third child. Dr Noel held up the third baby for the new dad's inspection.

'Doctor,' asked Paddy Joe, 'do you think it's the light that's attracting them?'

Hard times

The much-missed Labour TD for Limerick, Jim Kemmy, had an impoverished childhood. He remarked: 'It wasn't hard to tell we were poor – particularly when you saw the toilet paper drying on the clothesline.'

Commenting on how electricity had transformed Irish society, Kemmy joked: 'If it weren't for electricity we'd all be watching television by candlelight.'

Chapter 9 There's Something about Mary's Mob

In 1985, Des O'Malley founded the Progressive Democrats after he was expelled from Fianna Fáil for 'conduct unbecoming'. The PDs wanted to 'break the mould of Irish politics', and, in the words of Michael McDowell, would be 'radical or redundant'. The PDs made an immediate impact and polled well in the 1987 general election. As the following collection indicates, they have also brought smiles to the faces of some Irish political pundits.

Oh happy day
In 1999, the government jet was flying across the country with Bertie Ahern, Charlie McCreevy and Mary Harney on board.

Bertie looked out the window and said: 'I could throw a £100 note out the window right now and make someone very happy.'

Charlie said: 'I could throw ten £10 notes out the window and make ten people happy.'

Mary said: 'I could throw 100 £1 notes out the window and make 100 people happy.'

The pilot rolled his eyes to heaven and said softly: 'I could throw all three out the window and please the whole country.'

A bonnie baby
Mary Harney has not felt so ill since she became Minister for Health in 2004. It is a case of déjà flu.

Shortly after she became Minister for Health, Harney announced that she was reviewing government legislation in the area of IVF. This was on foot of the story of a 66-year-old woman who had given birth. Concerns grew after the woman was discharged from the hospital and went home. One day, her relatives came to visit.

'May we see the new baby?' one asked.

'Not yet,' said the mother. 'I'll make coffee and we can chat first.'

Thirty minutes passed, and another relative asked, 'May we see the baby now?'

'No, not yet,' replied the mother.

After another half an hour had elapsed, they asked again, 'May we see the baby now?'

'No, not yet,' replied the mother.

Growing very impatient, they asked, 'Well, when can we see the baby?'

'When it cries.'

'When it cries? Why do we have to wait until it cries?'

'Because I have forgotten where I put it.'

Wishing on a star

As Mary Harney was walking on a beach one day in February 2005, her foot tripped on a partially buried bottle. Picking it up, she rubbed it to expose the label. Suddenly a cloud poured from the bottle and a huge genie appeared.

'Thank you, oh thank you, for saving me from my prison. I've been in there for hundreds, yes, hundreds of years. As an expression of my overwhelming gratitude, I will grant you one wish.'

Facing yet another crisis in the peace process in the wake of stories about money laundering, Harney knew exactly what to ask for. 'A final political settlement in the North,' she quickly replied.

The genie seemed confused. 'The North...the North...I can't seem to remember...can you help me out a little?'

The Tanaiste quickly got on her mobile and had a world map sent over. She carefully pointed out the troubled area of the globe, recounting briefly the tortuous history of the peace process.

The genie's eyes widened and he said: 'Oh, yeah. Now I remember. The North! Whew. That's a tough one. Even stuck in my bottle, I know that they've been squabbling up there for decades. I hate to admit it, but I think that's more than I can handle. I'm sorry. Can you wish for something else?'

Mary, crestfallen at such a missed opportunity, could think of only one other wish: 'Could you make the Irish people like Michael McDowell?'

The genie paused, grimaced and then said, 'Let me see that map again.'

Heaven and earth

Bertie Ahern, Mary Harney and Michael McDowell all died in a plane crash. Upon reaching heaven, they were escorted as important personages directly to see God. God looked at Bertie and asked, 'Bertie, you've sinned a great deal. Why should I allow you to enter into heaven?'

'Well, God,' replied Bertie, 'I'm a true socialist and I redistributed the wealth of Ireland and gave it to the poor.'

God considered this a moment and said, 'Oh, okay. Sit over here on my left.' He turned to Mary. 'Mary, why should I let you into heaven?'

'Well, Lord, I got the smog out of Ireland in the late 1980s.'

God thought for a moment and said, 'All right. Sit over here on my right. Now, Michael, tell me why I should let you into heaven?'

'Well, God, it's like this. You're sitting on my seat.'

Marital discord

Michael McDowell's wife had not spoken to him in three days. It went back to an incident in the middle of the night when she thought she heard a noise downstairs.

She nudged him and whispered, 'Wake up, wake up!'

'What's the matter?' he asked.

'There are burglars in the kitchen. I think they're eating the beef casserole I made tonight.'

'That'll teach them,' he replied.

A Change of heart

The doctor told Michael McDowell he should start an exercise programme. He devised the following:

Beat around the bush;
Jump to conclusions;
Climb the walls;
Wade through the morning paper.

Drag my heels;
Push my luck;
Make mountains out of molehills;
Hit the nail on the head.

Bend over backwards;
Jump on the bandwagon;
Run around in circles.

Toot my own horn;
Pull out all the stops;
Add fuel to the fire.

Open a can of worms;
Put my foot in my mouth;
Start the ball rolling;
Go over the edge.

All donations gratefully received

A man on his way home from work was stuck in a traffic jam on Harcourt Street. He thought to himself, 'Wow, the traffic seems worse than usual. Nothing's moving.'

The man noticed a garda walking back and forth between the lines of cars, so he rolled down his window and asked, 'Excuse me, Guard, what's the problem?'

The officer replied, 'Michael McDowell just found out that Bertie Ahern is planning to get closer to Sinn Féin and he's depressed. He stopped his state car in the middle of the road, and he's threatening to douse himself in petrol and set himself on fire. He says Tom Parlon and Liz O'Donnell hate him, and he doesn't have any money since he built his holiday villa in Roscommon. I'm walking around doing a collection for him.'

'Oh, really. How much have you collected so far?'

'Well, people are still siphoning but right now I'd say about 300 litres.'

The Limerick Leader

Des O'Malley is a big racing fan. In 1982, he was all geared up to attend the Cheltenham Festival, but a general election intervened and at the last minute he had to cancel his trip to Cheltenham. He instructed his friend Danno Heaslip to put a bet on for him – £25 each way on Danno's horse, For Auction, in the Champion Hurdle. Danno went to Cheltenham on the Sunday, but before leaving posted a letter to O'Malley's home in Limerick, saying that so many people had asked him to back the horse that he couldn't possibly get it all on. For Auction won at 40–1. The only problem was that O'Malley had left for Dublin before the post arrived on the Monday morning and didn't get the letter until after the race – having already calculated that he had just won £1,250!

Leaving on a Jet Plane

A Fianna Fáil supporter, a Fine Gael supporter, a Labour Party supporter and a PD supporter are on a plane. The plane has too many people on it and is beginning to lose height. The Fine Gael supporter says, 'This is for you Enda Kenny,' and jumps off.

The Labour Party supporter says, 'This is for you Pat Rabbitte,' and jumps off.

Then the Fianna Fáil supporter says, 'This is for you Bertie,' and throws the PD off the plane.

Chapter 10 Power to All Our Friends

It is no use telling politicians to go to hell – they are trying to build it for us on earth.

Most of the stories in this chapter fall into the urban legend category. The following pages provide an entertaining tour through the continuous cock ups that make politics so unpredictable – and entertaining! Politics is often presented as a seamless garment, carefully wrought, but it is peopled by a motley crew of saints and sinners, geniuses and gombeens, eccentrics and experts. All shades of life are represented below in a series of light shafts into this strange world.

The unfab four

This is a story about the four most powerful people in politics, namely, Everybody, Somebody, Anybody and Nobody.

There was an important job to be done and Everybody was sure Somebody would do it.

Anybody could have done it, but Nobody did it.

Somebody got angry about that, because it was Everybody's job.

Everybody thought Anybody could do it, but Nobody realised that Everybody wouldn't do it.

It ended up that Everybody blamed Somebody but Nobody did what Anybody could have.

Holy cow

Politics can be very ideological. However, the ideologies can be very confusing. The following clarifies the issues:

Socialism: You have two cows, and you give one to your neighbour.

Communism: You have two cows, the government takes both of them and gives you the milk.

Fascism: You have two cows, the government takes both of them and sells you the milk.

Nazism: You have two cows, the government takes both of them and shoots you.

Capitalism: You have two cows, you sell one of them and buy a bull.

Irish politics: You have two cows, the government takes both of them, shoots one of them, milks the other and pours the milk down the drain.

Half full or half empty?

According to the well-known proverb: 'An optimist sees the glass as half full, while the pessimist would say it's half empty.'

Fianna Fáil would say that the glass is fuller than if the opposition were in power.

The Labour Party would say that it is irrelevant because the present administration has changed the way such volume statistics are collected.

Brian Cowen would say that, in real terms, the glass is 25 per cent fuller than at the same time last year.

The head of the Central Bank would say that the glass has just under 50 per cent of its net worth in liquid assets.

Anthony Clare would ask, 'What did your mother say about the glass?'

Colin Farrell would say that the glass doesn't have enough ice in it.

Theologically correct

A plane was about to crash in an isolated area. One of the passengers was lucky enough to find a parachute and escape. He landed on top of a very tall tree but had no idea where he was and was unable to move. After a while a man walked by. The parachutist shouted down, 'Excuse me, Sir. Do you know where I am?'

The man calmly replied, 'You're on top of a tree.'

The parachutist had a second question. 'By any chance are you a TD?'

The politician was astounded: 'Yes, I am. How could you guess?'

'It was very simple really. The information you gave me was absolutely correct but absolutely useless.'

Sleeping beauties

A teacher took her class on a trip to the Dáil. As they were on their way to the visitors' gallery she asked, 'Why is it necessary to be quiet in here?'

One bright little girl replied, 'Because people are sleeping.'

Clean cut

The local TD was suffering badly from insomnia. One day he met a friend and he told him his troubles.

The friend said, 'Why don't you take a hot whiskey before going to bed?'

'Oh,' replied the TD, 'I couldn't do that. Mary-Kate, my housekeeper, would tell the whole county.'

'Well,' said the friend, 'I'll tell you what to do. Just have your bottle of whiskey hidden in your room. Ask Mary-Kate for a cup of hot water, saying you want to shave.'

The TD did what his friend advised and had a great night's sleep. All went well until one day Mary-Kate was in the local shop and a customer asked her how her boss was getting on.

'To be honest,' said Mary-Kate, 'I think he's going soft in the head. He has shaved himself five times every day during the past week.'

Weighty matters

A 'calorifically challenged' TD said to one of his constituents, 'You only come up to my chin.'

The constituent replied, 'Which one?'

However, the TD was well able to laugh at himself. He once said, 'My circumference was built with a knife and fork.'

He was also a big fan of Alfred Hitchcock – as much for his self-deprecatory sense of humour as his films. Hitch said of his bulging waistline: 'I'm an expert on losing weight. I represent the survival of the fattest. Journalists often ask how much I weigh. I tell them, only once a day, before breakfast.' Hitchcock also revealed that on the set of his film *Lifeboat* 'a friend' told him that he would be just as unrecognisable floating face down as face up.

All the world's a stage

Amateur drama competitions are flourishing in Ireland. However, sometimes the real drama comes at the judging stage. A town in the south-east engaged the services of the local TD to judge a competition. The organisers had been led to believe that the TD was a great wit. On the night of the play, there was no escaping his caustic tongue. He took the packed audience by surprise by beginning his summation of a performance with an unusual question: 'Would anyone in this distinguished gathering have some onions?'

There was stunned silence before he continued: 'That's an awful shame. They would go exceptionally well with the tripe we have just been watching.'

There were one or two nervous titters. The TD struck an even more savage blow when giving the performers their marks.

'I am giving them 35 marks: 2 for finding the hall, 3 for getting the curtain up and 30 for mercifully getting the curtain down.'

An act of charity

The wife of a hen-pecked rural TD was chatting with her next-door neighbour. 'I feel really good today. I started out this morning with an act of unselfish generosity. I gave a €100 note to a bum.'

'You gave a bum €100? That's a lot of money to just give away. What did you husband say about it?'

'Oh, he thought it was the proper thing to do. He said, "Thanks".'

A no brainer

A TD found out that he had a brain tumour, and that it was inoperable. In fact, it was so large, they had to do a brain transplant. His doctor gave him a choice of available brains: there was a jar of rocket scientists' brains for €100 an ounce, a jar of dentists' brains for €150 an ounce and a jar of politicians' brains for €100,000 an ounce. The outraged TD said, 'This is a rip off! How come the politicians' brains are so damned expensive?' The doctor replied, 'Do you know how many politicians it takes to get an ounce of brains?'

Customer relations

Senator and Superquinn owner Feargal Quinn constantly preaches the gospel that the customer is always right. Sometimes quick thinking is required to keep customers placated. To illustrate he tells the story of the assistant in Superquinn who was gruffly greeted by a really rough looking customer in the fruit and vegetable section. The man wanted to buy half a lettuce. The assistant said, 'You can't buy half a lettuce. We only sell them whole.'

'Is that right?' asked the customer, tearing a lettuce in half and taking it to the checkout.

The cashier said he would have to check the price with the manager. He walked over to the manager and said, 'There's a dumb-looking ape out there who wants to buy half a lettuce.' Then he glanced back and saw that the tough customer had followed him, and had heard every word. He quickly continued, '…and this friendly customer offered to buy the other half.'

Quinn also tells another story of a difficult customer and a Superquinn manager. The conversation concluded as follows:

'Why do I never get what I ask for in this rotten shop?'

'Because, Madam, politeness is our motto.'

That sinking feeling

On Friday 13 June 2003, *Cabin Fever*, the ill-fated boat which was the basis for a reality television series on RTÉ, sank after colliding with rocks. To add to the ignominy, the camera crew were not on the ship at the time, so the most dramatic moments in the series were not captured on film. Having invested a small fortune in the series, RTÉ was forced to use amateur footage of the foundering of the ship. Vincent Browne saw the funny side of the events. He used it to make a political point by stating that rumours that the captain of *Cabin Fever* was in charge of Dublin transport were unfounded – *Cabin Fever* had only hit the rocks once.

Birdensome

In the run up to the 2002 general election, RTÉ political correspondent Charlie Bird was sitting beside a boy on an Aer Lingus flight to New York. As there was no film and he had no book with him, Charlie asked the boy if he would be interested in having a discussion with him about Bertie's chances in the election. 'Okay,' said the boy, 'that could be an interesting topic but let me ask you a question first. A horse, a cow and a deer all eat grass. The same stuff. Yet a deer excretes little pellets, while a cow turns out flat patties, and a horse excretes clumps of dried grass. Why do you think that is?'

'Jeez,' said Bird, 'I have no idea.'

'Well then,' said the boy, 'How is it you feel qualified to discuss who should run the country when you don't know s***?'

Lovely Leitrim

In August 2003 Leitrim got its first ever set of traffic lights. It was a major news story in the national media. Former presidential candidate Dustin the Turkey was heard to remark: 'Who even knew they had cars?'

Wishful thinking

David Norris tells the story of jazz musician George Melley's account of a piece of graffiti which read: 'My mother made me a homosexual.' Someone had written underneath it: 'If I bought the wool, would she make one for me?'

Lassie come home

In the 1990s, an Irish delegation was on a diplomatic tour of Cuba. After the politicians disembarked at Havana airport, they waited in the baggage hall, by the carousel. Bags went around and around, and the politicians waited patiently when they noticed a drugs squad officer with a sniffer dog in tow. The officer let the dog off the lead and it ran to the carousel and bounded onto the bags, rummaging around. One TD was awestruck: 'Isn't that wonderful?'

'Why?' asked his companion.

'Well, isn't it great, the dog is looking for the blind man's luggage.'

It's not the winning that counts...

In 1989, three Irish politicians were on a junket to Australia. On a day off, they were invited to the Royal Perth Yacht Club. It was just after Australia had lost to the US in the final of the Americas Cup yacht races. The president of the yacht club was showing the Irish politicians around the club and took them onto the *Kookaburra 2*, the boat that the hopes of the nation had rested on in the race. The captain of *Kookaburra 2* was then introduced to the TDs. One of the Irish innocently asked: 'Do a bit of racing then, do you?'

'Yeah, mate. In fact we've just been in the Americas Cup, where we sailed against the Americans.'

The second Irish man: 'How did you get on, then?'

'We came second.'

The third Irishman interjected: 'Second. That's bloody good, isn't it!'

Up the Pole

A delegation from Kildare Council was on tour of Poland. One evening, one of the councillors was in the back seat of a hired car in Warsaw. He was enjoying a few moments of bliss with his new girlfriend, when a policeman came up and shone his torch through the window.

'Do you know you're up a cul-de-sac?' asked the copper.

'Oh sorry, officer,' said the councillor. 'I just assumed that she was a Roman Catholic.'

A grave matter

A busload of Fianna Fáil politicians was driving down a country road in Kerry when, all of a sudden, the bus ran off the road and crashed into a tree in an old farmer's field. The farmer went over to investigate. He then dug a hole and buried the politicians.

A few days later, the local garda sergeant saw the crashed bus, and asked the farmer where all the politicians had gone. The old farmer said he had buried them. The garda then asked the old farmer, 'Were they all dead?' The old farmer replied, 'Well, some of them said they weren't, but you know them politicians lie.'

Lovestruck

A forlorn member of the Irish Communist Party trudged home after the polls closed in the 2002 general election.

'So, darling, how many votes did you get?' asked his wife.

'Three,' he responded.

She slapped him hard across the face.

'What was that for?' he asked.

'You have a mistress, now, do you?'

Healthy living

An administrator in the Department of Health sat in his office and, out of boredom, decided to see what was in his old filing cabinet. He poked through the contents and came across an old brass lamp. 'This will look nice on my mantelpiece,' he decided, and took it home with him.

While polishing the lamp, a genie appeared and granted him three wishes. 'I wish for an ice cold diet Coke right now.'

He got his Coke and drank it.

When he was more composed, the civil servant stated his second wish. 'I wish to be on an island where beautiful nymphomaniacs reside.' Suddenly he was on an island with gorgeous females eyeing him lustfully.

He told the genie his third and last wish. 'I wish I never had to work again.'

Poof! He was immediately transported back to his office in the Department of Health.

In the interest of efficiency

The Department of Health had a vast scrap yard in the middle of a bog. The Minister said, 'Someone may steal from it at night.' So they created a night watchman position and hired a man for the job at a salary of €35,000 a year.

Then the Department of Health's secretary wondered, 'How does the watchman do his job without instruction?' So they created a planning department and hired two people, one person to write the instructions and one person to do time studies. Then the secretary said, 'How are these people going to get paid?' So they hired two people to act as a timekeeper and a payroll officer.

Then the secretary asked, 'Who will be accountable for all of these people?' So they created an administrative section and hired three people, an administrative officer, assistant administrative officer and a legal secretary.

Then the Department of Health official said, 'We have had this command in operation for one year and we are €35,000 over budget. We must cutback overall costs.'

So they laid off the night watchman.

God versus the Green Party

God created heaven and earth. Quickly the Green Party faced him with a class action suit for failure to file an environmental impact statement. God was granted a temporary permit for the project, but was stymied with the cease and desist order for the earthly part.

Appearing at the hearing, God was asked why he had begun his earthly project in the first place. He replied that he just liked to be creative.

Then God said, 'Let there be light,' and immediately the Green Party demanded to know how the light would be made. Would there be strip mining? What about thermal pollution? God explained that the light would be made from a huge ball of fire. God was granted provisional permission to make light, assuming that no smoke would result from the ball of fire, that he would obtain a building permit and that, to conserve energy, he would turn the light off half the time. God agreed and said he would call the light 'Day' and the darkness 'Night'. The Green Party replied that they were not interested in semantics.

God said, 'Let the earth bear much seed.' The Greens agreed, so long as native seed was used. Then God said, 'Let waters bring forth creeping creatures begetting life; and the fowl that may fly over the earth.' The Green Party pointed out that this would require approval from the Society of the Prevention of Cruelty to Animals.

Everything was going fine until God said he wanted to complete the project in six days. The Green Party said it would take at least 200 days to review the application and impact statement. After that, there would be a public hearing. Then, there would be a 10–12-month approval period before…

At this point, God created hell.

Russian roulette

President of the Soviet Union, Leonid Brezhnev, was a big shooting fan. Once he went to visit a remote part of the USSR. The local secretary of the Communist Party was ordered to provide a bear for Brezhnev to shoot. The secretary was devastated because there were no bears in the area, but he was anxious to secure promotion so knew he had no option but to find a bear. Eventually he found a performing bear in the local circus. The bear was taken to the middle of the forest and placed on a track a mile and a half from where Brezhnev would be hiding with his rifle. The bear was then pushed off in the direction of Brezhnev.

Two minutes later a woodman was cycling home, and was stunned to be met by a bear. He fell off his bike with surprise and ran off into the forest. The bear was not phased. He picked up the bike and rode off along the path towards Brezhnev. Ten minutes later Brezhnev, with his rifle cocked, was astounded to see the bear cycling along. He was so surprised that his rifle went off and he shot himself in the foot.

Saints and sinners

In June 2005, the noted American cleric Cardinal Sin died. Back in the 1970s, the cardinal was invited to a dinner. The other guests were the President of the Philippines and his wife, Ferdinand and Imelda Marcos. Not being a fan of their ethics or their politics, Cardinal Sin took everyone by surprise when he said the grace before meals: 'Blessed are thou among sinners,' he pointedly remarked.

In 1992, Eamon Casey fled Ireland when news of his affair with Annie Murphy broke. It is rumoured that Casey sought out Cardinal Sin to hear his confession. When he went into the confessional box, Casey began by saying: 'Bless me Sin, for I have fathered.'

Eurosceptic

A committed Eurocrat went to the birth registration office to register his newborn son. The man behind the counter asked the name he wanted to give to the boy, and the father replied: 'Euro.'

The man said that such a name was not acceptable, because it is a currency. The Eurocrat replied: 'What? There weren't any objections when I called my first two sons Mark and Frank.'

Bumper stickers

Politicians are cleverly disguised as responsible adults.

If we quit voting, will they all go away?

How many roads must a politician travel down before he admits he is lost?

POLITICIANS & NAPPIES BOTH NEED TO BE CHANGED AND FOR THE SAME REASON.

A politician's dictionary

Most political speak induces a state of 'déjà moo' – the feeling that you've heard this bull before. However, the following is a reminder of what words really mean in political speak.

Yes. = No.

No. = Yes.

Maybe. = No.

I'm sorry. = You'll be sorry.

We need. = I want.

It's the voter's decision. = My correct decision should be obvious by now.

Do what you want. = You'll pay for this later.

We need to talk. = I need to complain.

Sure, go ahead. = I don't want you to.

I'm not upset. = Of course I'm upset, you moron.

On a wing and a prayer

A ship was sinking rapidly and a politician was nervously passing out the life jackets. He shouted out: 'Does anyone here know how to pray?' Immediately a man said: 'I do'.

The politician replied: 'Thank goodness for that – we're short one life jacket.'

Unfair trade

An African woman made an observation before the much-hyped Live 8 concert in July 2005. 'When the missionaries came to Africa, they had the Bible and we had the land. They said: "Let us pray." We closed our eyes. When we opened them, we had the Bible and they had the land.'

Career guidance

An older couple had a son who was still living with them. The parents were a little worried, as the son was still unable to decide about his career path. So they decided to do a little test. They took a €100 note, a Bible and a bottle of brandy, and put them on the front hall table. Then they hid in the nearby closet, hoping their son would think they weren't at home. The father told the mother, 'If he takes the money he will be a businessman, if he takes the Bible he will be a priest, but if he takes the bottle of whiskey, I'm afraid our son will be a drunkard.'

The parents waited nervously. Peeping through the keyhole they saw their son arrive home. He saw the note they had left, saying they'd be home later. Then he took the money, looked at it against the light, and slid it in his pocket.

After that, he picked up the Bible, flicked through it, and took it also. Finally, he grabbed the bottle, opened it, and took an appreciative whiff to be assured of the quality. Then he left for his room, carrying all three items. The father slapped his forehead, and said: 'Jaysus, it's even worse than I ever imagined…'

'What do you mean?' his wife inquired.

'Our son is going to be a politician!'

Doctor's orders

Five surgeons were discussing who makes the best patients for them to operate on. The first surgeon said: 'Accountants are the best to operate on because when you open them up, everything inside is numbered.'

The second responded, 'Try electricians. Everything inside them is colour coded.'

The third surgeon said, 'No, librarians are the best. Everything inside them is in alphabetical order.'

The fourth surgeon interceded, 'I like construction workers…they always understand when you have a few parts left over at the end and when it takes longer than you expect.'

To which the fifth surgeon said: 'You're all wrong. Politicians are the easiest. There's no guts, no heart no spine and their heads and arses are interchangeable.'

Chapter 11 Our Friends Up North

Since the Troubles began, there have been more tears than laughter in Northern Ireland. The rich history of Irish literature is filled with stories of hatred, division and violence from that troubled part of the world. To date, though, there has been precious little written on the comic side of the Troubles. This chapter assembles some of the few funny stories that have emerged from the darkest chapter of Irish political history.

A different emphasis

How would you react if a man with a knife threatened your life not knowing that you were armed with a gun?

A member of the SDLP: 'Well, that's not enough information to answer the question. Does the man look poor or oppressed? Have I ever done anything that would inspire him to attack? Could we run away? What does my wife think? Could I possibly swing the gun like a club and knock the knife out of his hand? Why am I carrying a loaded gun anyway, and what kind of message does this send to society and to my children? We need to raise taxes and make this a happier, healthier society that would discourage such behaviour. This is all so confusing. I need to debate this with my party colleagues for a few days and come to some kind of consensus.'

A member of Sinn Féin: BANG! BANG! BANG! BANG! BANG! BANG! BANG!…click…(sounds of reloading)…BANG! BANG! BANG! BANG! BANG! BANG! BANG!

Warning

At the height of the IRA bombing campaign in the 1980s, an Irishman arrived up at the pearly gates, and patiently waited for St Peter to look up from his work. Finally, Peter gave the Irishman his attention.

'And you are?' St Peter asked.

'I'm Séamus Kelly,' replied the Irishman.

'Hmm, Kelly…Kelly…,' the gatekeeper mused, pouring over his compendious list of people and events. 'Ah, here were are. Séamus Kelly…you're a member of the IRA.'

'Yeah, that'd be me,' replied Kelly.

'You blew up that pub in Manchester.'

'Yeah.'

'You also blew up the car of a judge in Belfast, killing him and his two young children.'

'Yeah, that's all my work.'

St Peter was amazed at Kelly's cheek, and when he finally found words he blurted, 'Well, good God, man, we just can't let you in here.'

'Let me in?' said Kelly. 'Hell, I've just come to tell you you've got ten minutes to get out.'

On time

The IRA imposed a 10 o'clock curfew in Belfast. Everybody had to be off the streets or would risk being shot. However, one citizen was shot at 9.45 pm.

'Why did you do that?' the volunteer was asked by his superior officer.

'I know where he lives,' he replied, 'and he wouldn't have made it.'

A bridge over troubled waters

One day, Gerry Adams was out jogging, and accidentally fell from a bridge into a very cold river. Three boys, playing along the river, saw the accident. Without a second thought, they jumped in the water and dragged the wet Sinn Féin President out of the river. After cleaning up, Adams said, 'Boys, you saved the architect of the peace process today. You deserve a reward. You name it, I'll give it to you.'

The first boy said, 'I'd like a ticket to Disneyland, please.'

'I'll personally hand it to you,' said Adams.

'I'd like a U2 CD,' the second boy asked.

'I'll buy it myself and give it to you,' Adams replied.

'And I'd like a wheelchair with a stereo in it,' said the third boy.

'I'll personally...wait a second, son, you're not disabled.'

'No, but my father is a member of the DUP. He'll put me in a wheelchair when he finds out who I saved from drowning.'

Mighty Mo

In August 2005, the death of Mo Mowlam saddened the political world in Northern Ireland and beyond. Mo was one of the main architects of the Good Friday Agreement. She was an unusual woman – her idea of a gift for John and Pat Hume's new weekend home was a year's supply of toilet roll!

During her time as Northern Ireland secretary, Mo addressed a group of librarians in Bangor. She spoke enthusiastically about the importance of libraries to children. Mo concluded her talk by saying: 'As a child, a library card takes you to exotic, faraway places. When you are grown up, a credit card does that.'

Mo also spoke to a women's group in Derry, and talked movingly about her experiences recovering from a brain tumour. Her unusual take on therapy brought the house down: 'Being in therapy is great. I spend an hour just talking about myself. It's kind of like being the man on a date.'

The plain truth

George Bush was looking to hide Saddam Hussein in a place where he would never be found. So he hid him in the Sinn Féin office for straight talking.

Chapter 12 New Computer Viruses

Computer experts have advised all PC owners to immediately scan their computers for the following viruses.

Michael McDowell Virus:

Your system works fine, but complains loudly about foreign software.

Mary Harney Virus:

Makes its presence known but doesn't do anything. Secretly, you wish it would.

Micheál Martin Virus:

Files disappear, only to reappear mysteriously a year later, in another directory.

IRA Virus:

You know it's guilty of trashing your system, but you just can't prove it.

Michael Noonan Virus:

Could be virulent, but it's been around too long to be much of a threat.

Politically Correct Virus:

Never identifies itself as a 'virus', but instead refers to itself as an 'electronic micro-organism'.

Martin Cullen Virus:

Activates every component in your system, just before the whole thing quits.

Government Economist Virus:

Nothing works, but all your diagnostic software says everything is fine.

Gerry Adams Virus:

Probably harmless, but it makes a lot of people really mad just thinking about it.

Government Virus:

Divides your hard disk into hundreds of little units, each of which does practically nothing; but all of which claim to be the most important part of your computer.

The Red Hand of Ulster Virus:

Screen changes colour every time it boots up and head butts you or kicks you in the groin when you attempt to remove it.

Coalition Virus:

The computer locks up and the screen splits in half with the same message appearing on each side. The message says that the blame for the gridlock is caused by the other side.

VHI Virus:

Your program stops running every few minutes to ask for more money.

The MRBI Virus:

60% of the PCs infected will lose 44% of their data 17% of the time (plus or minus a 3.5 % margin of error).

The Freedom of Information Act Virus:

Causes your printer to become a paper shredder.

Health Care Consultant Virus:

Tests your system for a day, finds nothing wrong and sends you a bill for €10,000 a day.

Government Spokesperson Virus:

Nothing works but the system constantly reassures you that everything is fine.

Chapter 13 Love Stories

It's a well-kept secret that Irish politicians have been known to give cupid's arrow a helping hand. Charlie Haughey was asked to give advice to a woman who wanted an increase in the widows' pension. He replied, 'Get married again!'

Haughey's definition of a honeymoon is: 'The vacation a man takes before going to work for a new boss.'

In fact, sex has cast a shadow over the Irish body politic. In March 1991, an *Irish Press* headline stated: 'PDs Split on Condoms'.

At the time, Fine Gael TD Bernard Durkan stated, 'Over 155 million condoms have been imported into Ireland in recent years. Either a lot of people are using them or some fellow out there is making an awful animal of himself.' Years earlier Jack Lynch had famously said, 'I would not like to leave contraception on the long finger for too long.'

Asked to explain the difference between northsiders and southsiders, Brian Lenihan joked, 'A northside woman has fake jewellery and real orgasms; with a southside woman it's just the opposite.'

The love machine

It is not widely known but Micheál Martin is the most romantic member of the current cabinet. On the night of his wedding anniversary, Micheál sat his wife down in the living-room with her favourite magazine, turned on the soft reading lamp, slipped off her shoes, patted and propped her feet. Then, he went into the kitchen to prepare dinner.

'How romantic,' she thought.

Two and a half hours later, she was still waiting for dinner to be served. She tiptoed to the kitchen and found it in a colossal mess. Her harried husband, removing something indescribable from the smoking oven, saw her in the doorway. 'Almost ready!' he vowed. 'Sorry it took me so long but I had to refill the pepper shaker.'

'Why, honey, how long could that have taken you?'

'More than an hour, I reckon. Wasn't easy stuffing it through those stupid little holes.'

Every rose has its thorns

All marriages are happy. It's the living together afterwards that causes all the trouble. Martin's wife accused him of loving politics more than her. 'Yeah, but I love you more than hurling or rugby,' he replied.

In fairness, she did pay him a great compliment. She told him that he brought 'a little ray of sunshine' into her life. He was chuffed and asked her how. She took the wind out of his sails when she answered: 'When you came home last night foaming at the mouth and muttering something about the former Secretary of the Department of Health, you slammed the door so hard that the venetian blind fell off the window.'

Micheál's wife asked him to bring her out for a meal. He rang several restaurants, the first four of which were fully booked. He did find a place that could take them. 'I'm not going there,' said Mrs Martin. 'It can't be much good if it isn't full.'

Effective tactics

On Valentine's Day, Séamus Brennan, Micheál Martin and a cabinet colleague assembled for a round of golf. All three were quite surprised at having been able to escape from their wives for the day, and so compared notes on how they managed it. Séamus Brennan said, 'I bought my wife a dozen red roses, and she was so surprised and touched that she let me go.'

Micheál Martin said, 'I bought my wife a diamond ring, and she was so thrilled that she let me go.'

Their colleague said, 'Last night I had a big feed of garlic. When I woke up this morning, I rolled on top of my wife, breathed with gusto into her face and asked, "Golf course or intercourse?" She blinked and replied, "I'll put your clubs in the car".'

Foreplay

Enda Kenny is a keen sports fan. At a dull party, he approached a very attractive young woman and propositioned her in an unusual way, 'Would you ever chat to me for a minute or two? United are playing on television tonight and if my wife sees me talking to you, she'll decide that it's time to go home.'

Swept off her feet

The former Fine Gael TD for Donegal, Jim White, doubled up as a matchmaker. He told the story of Bashful Brian in Leitrim, who asked Mary to propose to her sister Molly for him, while he stood behind the back door of the cottage. 'If I'm good enough to be married,' Molly answered, 'I'm good enough to be asked.' So the ageing Romeo opened the door and said, 'Will you do what your sister asked?'

Another of Jim's stories went back to the time in rural Ireland when women regularly had arranged marriages. Often they got more than they bargained for. Two old bachelor brothers, Willie and Tommy, were inseparable. Then Willie suddenly decided to get married, much to Tommy's chagrin. However, the wedding went ahead and on the bride's first morning in her new home, the brothers were out, as usual, milking the cows and feeding the pigs and chickens. After the tasks were completed, Tommy was first into the kitchen, and on seeing no sign of a breakfast, he pushed open the bedroom door and shouted, 'Will you get up to hell outta that or what did we marry you for?'

White also relates the story about the queue in heaven. There was a door outside heaven with a notice: 'All henpecked husbands queue here.' A vast queue stretched to infinity. A few yards along there was another door with the notice: 'All husbands who lived in peace and contentment queue here.'

One tiny, timid man stood outside. The angel on duty came up to him and asked: 'Why are you standing here?' 'I don't know, really,' he laughed nervously. 'The wife told me to!'

Can I have my money back?

After delivering an inspiring homily during the ten o'clock Mass, the parish priest was delighted when a prominent Fianna Fáil TD asked him if he could talk to him about his sermon. The priest brought him back to his office and over coffee they settled down for a chat. The man asked, 'In your homily, Father, you said it was wrong for people to profit from other people's mistakes. Do you really agree with that?'

The cleric replied, 'Of course I do.'

'In that case will you consider refunding the 20 quid I paid you for marrying me to my wife seven years ago?'

A change of heart

The former Fine Gael Minister Peter Barry tells the story of two women he overheard talking on the train. One said, 'I went to a wedding this weekend but I don't think the marriage will last.'

'Why not?' asked the other.

'When the bride said, "I do," the groom told her, "Don't use that tone of voice with me".'

Hope springs eternal

A former Fianna Fáil TD went to his doctor and told him that he wanted a vasectomy. 'This is quite serious,' said the doctor. 'Have you discussed it with your wife?'

'Oh, yes,' he replied. 'She agrees.'

'And your children?'

'Yes,' said the man. 'They're in favour – 18 to 4.'

Not for better or worse

A young TD was in love with two women and could not decide which of them to marry. Finally, he went to a marriage counsellor. When asked to describe his two loves, he noted that one was a great poet and the other made delicious pancakes.

'Oh,' said the counsellor, 'I see what the problem is. You can't decide whether to marry for batter or verse.'

The absent-minded professor

During the 1982 general election, Garrett Fitzgerald was caught wearing odd shoes. His excuse was that he had dressed himself in the dark to avoid waking his wife, Joan. Shortly afterwards, a joke did the rounds that highlighted Garrett's absent-mindedness. One night, a gushing female approached Garrett at a dinner party. 'Don't you remember me, Garrett?' she said.

'I'm afraid not.'

'Well, many years ago you asked me to marry you,' she said.

'Really? And did you?'

All's not fair in love and war

Dick Spring tells the story of how he dumped one of his first girlfriends. She had given him an ultimatum: shave your moustache or lose me. He thought it was unfair because she had a moustache of her own!

Cautious

A Fianna Fáil TD believed in responsible sex. He made passionate love during the safe period – when his wife was away.

Is small beautiful?

An unusually 'small' Fianna Fáil TD, who rejoiced in the nickname 'the jockey', fancied himself as a ladies' man. He took his girlfriend to a hotel for a night of illicit pleasure, and they both took off their clothes. She took one look at his 'tackle' and said: 'Just who do you expect to satisfy with that?'

'Me!' he replied.

Lovestruck

The combination of heavy drinking and a search for romance was to the fore when a group of Kerry councillors were on a junket in Edinburgh. One night, they heard a rumour that there were a number of pretty Scottish nurses locked up in a local hostel. After closing time they climbed over the walled gate and crept stealthily up to the windows. Just when they reached their vantage point, a large matron came to the window and they made a hasty retreat. They decided to wait outside until the matron went to bed, only to discover that she had rung the police. They were introduced to the Scottish accent in all its glory when a big police officer said, or appeared to say, to them: 'Well, ma wee laddies w'a do you think ye're doing here at this hor of the nigt?'

'I'm sorry, Sir, we got lost.'

'Listen, laddies, we all know 'tis the nurses ye're after but let me tell ye one thing. Ye're making a fierce mistake. They're the ugliest lot you ever saw!'

Downsizing

Losing a place at the cabinet table really changes a politician's life. One former minister came home one evening and said to his wife, 'I think you'd better learn how to cook, my dear, because we're going to have to get rid of the cook. And you'd better learn to clean the house, because we'll have to get rid of the cleaning lady.'

'Okay,' said his wife, 'but you'd better learn to make love, so we can fire the chauffeur, too.'

Some mothers do have them

Strangely for a politician, a Fianna Fáil TD was a complete innocent. He asked his mother for advice on what to do on his wedding night. 'Well, son,' said his mother, 'you simply put your…you know…the hardest part of yourself into her…into the place where she wee-wees.' At the honeymoon hotel that night, the couple had to call for an ambulance. The TD had got his head stuck in a chamber pot.

What becomes of the broken-hearted?

A Cumann chairman was having a cup of tea in the local pub before a meeting. 'Why are you looking so glum, Séamus?' asked the landlord.

'My wife ran off with my best friend last night,' replied the local TD.

'Oh no,' said the landlord, 'that's bad news.'

'You're not wrong,' said the TD. 'He was meant to be my election agent.'

A grave matter

On election day, voters were approaching the polling station when a funeral procession went past. Seeing this, a Fianna Fáil TD took off his hat and stood motionless for a moment before walking on. 'That was a nice thing to do,' said his friend.

'Well,' said the TD, 'she was a good wife to me.'

One moment in time

A so-called political widow was having a go at her husband. 'Your whole life is politics,' she moaned. 'You never take me out, you never buy me presents. You're either at a meeting or watching politics on the telly. I bet you can't even remember when our wedding anniversary is.'

'Yes, I can,' replied the husband, 'it's 24 June, the same date that I was first elected to the county council.'

A dying wish

Queen Caroline, the wife of King George II, lay on her deathbed, while her husband knelt beside her, wringing his hands in studied grief. She urged him to marry again.

'Never,' he replied. 'I will always take mistresses.'

'That should not hamper your marrying.'

Strange but true

A former leader of the Conservative Party gave advice to his male cabinet members: 'Never get caught in bed with a live man or a dead woman.'

Sex, please we're British

During World War II, it was reported to Winston Churchill that, early one winter's morning, a retired admiral had been caught with a call girl in St James's Park. 'Now,' said Churchill, 'let's get this straight. Are you saying he was actually with a young girl at six in the morning with frost on the grass? And that he was 75?' The details were confirmed.

'By God,' laughed Churchill, 'makes one proud to be British.'

Sadly some British politicians do not celebrate love and sex with the same gusto as Churchill. They are so cynical that when they smell flowers they go looking for a coffin. Former Prime Minister Benjamin Disraeli famously said, 'My idea of an agreeable person is a person who disagrees with me.' On being told that a couple was getting married because they loved each other, Disraeli remarked, 'I wanted a reason, and you gave me an excuse.'

Another leading British political figure, Sir Alan Herbert, described marriage as, 'Holy Deadlock'. However, the most damning of all was Lord Chesterfield. Writing to his illegitimate son about sex, he stated, 'The pleasure is momentary; the position ridiculous; and the expense damnable.'

Ladies' man

A British MP was a big hit with women. During World War II, he was an army officer and had an affair with a Danish nymphomaniac. He sent her a telegram to say that he had two days' leave. It read: 'Arriving Wednesday. Will come straight to flat with secret weapon.' When he arrived at the flat he found M15 officers waiting to inspect his military hardware.

Up to his neck in it

The late Tory minister Alan Clark was a notorious womaniser and serial adulterer. He once said that his speciality was: 'Women and other diseases.' One Christmas, his wife went into the men's section of a department store to buy a white dress shirt for her husband. When the shop assistant asked about his collar size, Mrs Clark looked puzzled at first, then her face brightened. She held up her hands, forming a circle with her forefingers and thumbs.

'I don't know his size,' she said, 'but my hands fit perfectly around his neck.'

Non-fatal distraction

Former minister and John Major's erstwhile lover, Edwina Currie was asked by a businessman for advice on precautions against catching AIDS abroad: 'Take the wife. Failing that, take a good book,' she replied.

Chapter 14 The Best of British

Politics in the UK is full of British reserve and all that goes with the tradition of the 'stiff upper lip'. Yet, as we are about to see, hidden in the undergrowth of British politics, there lies a unique culture which has produced a few comic episodes. This chapter will do nothing to improve your political instincts, but it will make you smile.

The good joke guide

Tony Blair to William Hague: 'At least my jokes are proper ones.'
Hague: 'All your jokes are in the cabinet.'

Situation not vacant

Once there was a rumour that Tony Blair was thinking of becoming a Catholic. A friend asked him if there was any truth in it.

'Certainly not,' said Blair. 'They've already got a Pope.'

Nationality

Tony Blair, Jacques Chirac and Vladimir Putin were viewing a painting of Adam and Eve frolicking in the Garden of Eden.

'Look at their reserve, their calm,' mused Blair. 'They must be British.'

'Nonsense,' Chirac disagreed. 'They're naked, and so beautiful. Clearly, they are French.'

'No clothes, no shelter,' Putin pointed out, 'they have only an apple to eat, and they're being told this is paradise. They are definitely Russian.'

Blind date

Britain's Deputy Prime Minister John Prescott is famous for his short temper. During the 2001 general election, he was famously accosted by a disgruntled voter. In the full glare of the media, Prescott punched him in the face.

Prescott is not known for his handsome features. When Prescott was a young man his friend, Joe, set him up on a blind date with a young lady friend of his. But Prescott was a little worried about going out with someone he had never seen before. 'What do I do if she's really unattractive? I'll be stuck with her all night.'

'Don't worry,' Joe said, 'just go and meet her first. If you like what you see, then everything goes as planned. If you don't just shout "Aaaaaauuuuuugggghhhh!" and fake an asthma attack.'

So that night, Prescott knocked at the girl's door and when she came out he was awe-struck at how attractive she was. He was about to speak when the girl suddenly shouted: 'Aaaaaaauuuuuuggggghhh!'

A scary visit

Michael Howard had the thankless task of leading the Conservative Party into the 2005 general election. Even some of his own supporters felt he was the wrong man for the job, with many believing that there was something sinister about his appearance. Labour supporters were more preoccupied by this and told the following story.

One bright, beautiful Sunday morning, everyone in a town outside London woke up early and went to their local church. Before the service started, the townspeople sat in their pews and talked about their lives and families.

Suddenly, Satan appeared at the altar. Everyone started screaming and running for the front entrance, trampling each other in their determined efforts to get away from Evil Incarnate.

Soon, everyone was evacuated from the church except for one woman, who sat calmly in her pew. She was seemingly oblivious to the fact that God's ultimate enemy was in her presence. As a keen reader of the English tabloid press, the Devil recognised her immediately as the wife of Michael Howard. Her indifference to his appearance confused the Devil a bit.

Satan walked up to her and said, 'Hey, don't you know who I am?'
The woman said, 'Yes, I sure do.'
Satan asked, 'Well, aren't you afraid of me?'
The woman said, 'Nope, I sure amn't.'
The Devil, perturbed, asked, 'And why aren't you afraid of me?'
'Well, I've been married to your brother for 25 years.'

Brute force

Former Conservative MP and author Jeffrey Archer was having his
plush home redecorated. A tradesman had spent hours laying a carpet
specially imported from Pakistan in one of the guest rooms. He
decided to take a well-earned break and have a cigarette. He put his
hand in his pockets, but couldn't find his cigarettes. Then, to his
horror, he saw a lump in the middle of the carpet. 'Oh, no!' he
thought. 'I'm not going to take up all the carpet for a packet of fags.'
So he got a hammer and flattened the lump. Just then, Mary Archer
came into the room, holding the missing packet of cigarettes. 'I think
these must be yours', she said. 'I don't smoke. Filthy habit. And by the
way, you haven't seen my pet hamster, have you?'

The future king and I

In the 1990s there was much media speculation about the doomed
romance between Princess Diana and England's rugby captain Will
Carling. Carling strongly denied the rumours. After news of the
alleged affair was leaked to the press, Prince Charles had to present
the International Championship trophy to Carling, after a match in
which the captain failed to get a try. The prince said, 'I'm sorry you
didn't score.'

Carling replied: 'At last. Somebody believes me.'

Hanging loose

After England's Grand Slam victory against France at Twickenham in
1991, Mick 'the Munch' Skinner decided to take an early bath so that
he could go on the beer undisturbed. The President of the RFU
escorted Prime Minister John Major, an enthusiastic rugby fan, into
the dressing-room to congratulate the winning team. The first person

they met was a naked Mick Skinner with a towel in his left hand and his 'privates' in his right. The Munch held out his right hand and in his best Geordie accent said: 'Yo, John. Top man, large, bosh, put it there. How it's hanging?' Despite knowing where Skinner's right hand had just been, the PM shook it without any apparent qualms and retorted: 'Obviously not as well as you, Mr Skinner.'

A variation of the story has Skinner greeting Prince William in the home dressing-room before an England international at Twickenham. Prince William offered his hand in handshake and Skinner shook it and said: 'Afternoon, Sir. How's it hanging?'

After the next home match, Prince William was again brought into the England dressing-room to congratulate the victorious team. When he was reintroduced to Skinner, he said: 'Well done, Mr Skinner. And before you ask, may I inform you it's hanging very well.'

A moment to cherish

Micheál O'Muircheartaigh is a universally loved broadcaster. He is completely free from the pretension associated with many of his colleagues. Not for him the epigraph given to one of his peers, 'The ego has landed'.

In his broadcasting career Micheál has found evidence that, if horse racing is the sport of kings, greyhound racing is the sport of princes. Micheál was the first Irish journalist to interview a British royal, Prince Edward, on RTÉ radio. As joint owner of the greyhound Druid's Johnno, Prince Edward was celebrating his semifinal victory in the English Greyhound Derby at Wimbledon. Micheál stepped up and asked in his velvety soft tones, as only he can, 'Now tell me, Prince'.

A royal performance

At Epsom in 2000, two male streakers decided to reveal all in front of the Queen Mother. The official line was, 'We are not amused'. However, the next day the tabloids published photos of the Queen Mother gazing intently at the two men through her binoculars.

Routine

A while ago, Prince Philip flew into a local airport, to attend a public function in the neighbourhood. When he descended the steps from the plane, he was met by the leader of the reception committee. Unable to think of anything better to say, the wretched man asked how the prince's flight had been.

'Have you ever flown in a plane?' Philip responded.

'Oh, yes, your Royal Highness, often.'

'Well, it was just like that.'

The fortune cookie

In 1990, Margaret Thatcher went to a fortune teller and asked her when she was going to die. The fortune teller looked deeply into her crystal ball and said: 'You will die on a national holiday.'

'Oh really?' said Maggie. 'Which one?'

'Any day you die will be a national holiday.'

Late in his life Mrs Thatcher's husband, Denis, was found reading the Bible. When asked why, he quoted W.C. Fields, 'I'm looking for loopholes'.

The bitter truth

Although she was not a Catholic, Margaret Thatcher thought she had better take out spiritual insurance and went to confession: 'Father, I was looking in a mirror and I decided I was beautiful. Was this a terrible sin?' The priest answered: 'Certainly not. It was just a terrible mistake.'

The Iron Lady

Margaret Thatcher was a no-nonsense politician. While she was Prime Minister, cabinet responsibility generally involved agreeing with her. She famously said, 'I don't mind how much my ministers talk as long as they do what I say.' Interviewed in the US in 1991, Maggie underlined that politics had priority in her life, 'Home is the place you go to when you have nothing better to do'.

Big Maggie was not renowned for her feminist sensibilities. When the Iron Lady became Tory leader, Barbara Castle said, 'She is clearly the best man among them'. She was also known for speaking her mind. In 1989, Denis Healy said, 'Mrs Thatcher tells us she has given the French President a piece of her mind…not a gift I would receive with alacrity.'

Geoffrey Howe was one of the Iron Lady's cabinet ministers. Howe once lost his trousers on a train, and was told by a colleague, 'I was thrilled about the loss of your trousers because it revealed your human face'.

Waspish

Michael Heseltine was another of Thatcher's ministers. Heseltine was not, to use a euphemism, a close ally of Maggie. He said, 'They say a man should be judged by his enemies. I am very proud of mine.' Heseltine had an interesting political memory. 'I am humble enough to recognise that I have made mistakes, but politically astute enough to know that I have forgotten what they are.'

Heseltine took no prisoners. Reacting to the appointment of a Labour minister he said, 'Putting him in the cabinet is like appointing Dracula to take charge of the blood transfusion service.'

Neil Kinnock said of Heseltine, 'If I was in the gutter, which I am not, he'd still be looking up at me from the sewer.'

Dear John

John Major had the reputation of being the greyest and dullest Prime Minister in British history. However, people radically revised their assessment of him, after it emerged that he had had an affair with Edwina Currie. In the wake of the revelation, a story surfaced that Major had collapsed and was rushed to hospital. While he was in intensive care and his face was covered by an oxygen mask, he asked a nurse: 'Have my testicles turned black?' Startled, the nurse fumbled around under the blanket before reassuring him. Major pulled off his mask. 'That was delightful, nurse. But tell me, have my results come back?'

Internal combustion

The British Labour Party has a long tradition of internal division. Harold Wilson said, 'I have always said of Tony [Benn] that he immatures with age.' However, there is a great history of banter between the British parties. The classic is probably Harold Macmillan's: 'As usual the Liberals [the old Liberal Party] offer a mixture of sound and original ideas. Unfortunately none of the sound ideas is original, and none of the original ideas is sound.'

Neil Kinnock once unexpectedly found himself out-quipped by John Major. To rebuke the former Labour leader, the Tory quoted Shakespeare, 'You draweth out the thread of your verbosity finer than the staple of your argument.'

During the 1992 election campaign, a demonstrator threw an egg at John Major and splattered his suit. Asked by the media to comment, Major replied, 'Some people eat eggs, I wear them.'

Sex, lies and strange shape

It was said of Winston Churchill, 'I thought he was a young man of promise; but it appears he was a young man of promises'. Churchill himself defined the attributes of a successful politician, 'Political skill is the ability to foretell what is going to happen...and to have the ability afterwards to explain why it did not happen.' He also shared his thoughts on obsessives: 'A fanatic is one who can't change his mind and won't change the subject.'

Winston Churchill was very critical of the failings of his opponents. Discussing the merits of the Labour leader, Clement Attlee, a colleague said to Churchill:

'At least you'll have to admit that he's very modest.'

'Absolutely true,' agreed Churchill, 'but then he does have a lot to be modest about.'

Surprisingly, it was not Churchill but one of Attlee's own party members who said, 'An empty taxi drew up at the House of Commons, and Mr Attlee stepped out.'

Aneurin Bevan, a consistent adversary of Churchill's, said of one of Churchill's speeches, 'The mediocrity of his thinking is concealed only by the majesty of his language'.

However, Churchill was not a man to let an opponent have the last word. The Liverpool MP Bessie Braddock exclaimed, 'Winston, you're drunk.'

'Bessie, you're ugly,' replied Churchill, 'but tomorrow, I shall be sober.'

Churchill seems to have been the recipient of more than his fair share of female resentment. One evening at dinner, Churchill, who had recently grown whiskers, was berated by a female guest. 'Mr Churchill, I care neither for your politics nor your moustache,' she complained.

'Do not distress yourself,' he told her, 'you are very unlikely to come into contact with either.'

When Churchill was 75, he was asked whether he had any fear of death. 'I am ready to meet my Maker. But whether my Maker is prepared for the great ordeal of meeting me is another matter.'

An ardent admirer of Keir Hardie's told Churchill, 'He is not a great politician, but he will be in heaven before you or me, Winston.' To which Churchill replied, 'If heaven is going to be filled with people like Hardie, well the Almighty can have them to himself.'

When George Bernard Shaw's play *Saint Joan* opened in London, Shaw sent Churchill two tickets for the opening night. Enclosed with the tickets was a brief note saying, 'One for yourself and one for your friend, if you have one.' Churchill returned the tickets, saying that he would be unable to attend, but added that he wouldn't mind tickets for the second night, 'if there is one'.

Churchill hated any kind of pretension. He once said of Stafford Cripps, a politician of great austerity, unmatched piety and rigid teetotalism: 'There but for the grace of God, goes God.'

Tactless

Winston Churchill was having a chat with a publisher at a launch party. Out of the corner of his eye, he noticed a sartorially challenged woman. He turned to the publisher and pointed to the female and asked: 'Who on earth is that wretched-looking woman over there?' As soon as he saw the look on his publisher's face, he immediately knew that the woman was the publisher's wife.

The Lord knows

A keen fan of the ageing Winston Churchill asked him what he meant by a particular image in one of his speeches. 'When I wrote it,' Churchill replied, 'only two people knew the significance – myself and God. Now only God knows.'

Appearances can be deceptive

During Harold Macmillan's time as Prime Minister, he received a grave message about a diplomatic disaster. BBC radio reported the event as follows: 'These dismal tidings were delivered to the PM on the golf course, where he was playing a round with Lady Dorothy.' The words read fine in print but, when spoken, the sentence took on a very different connotation!

The first lady

Nancy Astor was the first woman to sit in the House of Commons. She became known for her quick wit on the hustings. Challenged by a farm worker as to her knowledge of rural affairs, she demanded that he ask her a question.

'Well then, how many toes has a pig got?' he asked.

'You take off your boot, my man, and count them,' she replied.

Astor had a keen awareness of her own foibles: 'I am the kind of woman I would run away from.' She was also very honest: 'The only thing I like about rich people is their money.'

Lloyd George once asked Lady Astor, 'What are you doing with my secretary, Philip Kerr?' To which she replied indignantly, 'Absolutely nothing.'

'Then,' replied Lloyd George, 'You ought to be ashamed of yourself.'

Cultural differences explained

Aussies: Dislike being mistaken for Brits when abroad.
Canadians: Are rather indignant about being mistaken for Americans when abroad.
Americans: Encourage being mistaken for Canadians when abroad.
Brits: Can't possibly be mistaken for anyone else when abroad.

Aussies: Believe you should look out for your mates.
Brits: Believe that you should look out for those people who belong to your club.
Americans: Believe that people should look out for and take care of themselves.
Canadians: Believe that's the government's job.

Aussies: Are extremely patriotic to their beer.
Americans: Are flag-waving, anthem-singing and obsessively patriotic.
Canadians: Can't agree on the words to their anthem, when they can be bothered to sing it.
Brits: Do not sing at all but prefer a large brass band to perform the anthem.

Americans: Spend most of their lives glued to the idiot box.
Canadians: Don't watch much TV, but only because they can't get more American channels.
Brits: Pay a tax just so they can watch four channels.
Aussies: Export all their crappy programmes, which no one there watches, to Britain, where everybody loves them.

Americans: Will jabber on incessantly about American football, baseball and basketball.
Brits: Will jabber on incessantly about cricket, soccer and rugby.
Canadians: Will jabber on incessantly about hockey, hockey, and how they beat the Americans twice, playing baseball.

Aussies: Will jabber on incessantly about how they beat the Brits in every sport they play them in.

Brits: Shop at home and have goods imported because they live on an island.
Aussies: Shop at home and have goods imported because they live on an island.
Americans: Cross the southern border for cheap shopping, gas and booze in a backward country.
Canadians: Cross the southern border for cheap shopping, gas and booze in a backward country.

Americans: Seem to think that poverty and failure are morally suspect.
Canadians: Seem to think that wealth and success are morally suspect.
Brits: Seem to believe that wealth, poverty, success and failure are inherited.
Aussies: Seem to think that none of this matters after several beers.

Chapter 15 Quote, Unquote

One lesson politicians have sadly never learned is that, when you are in deep water, it is a good idea to keep your mouth shut. As a result, they have talked themselves into trouble more often than most people have hot dinners.

The definition that I feel best sums up some politicians is the late Peter Ustinov's: 'Someone who searches for ages for the wrong word, which to his eternal credit he invariably finds.' If there is a wrong word to be found, you can bet your bottom dollar politicians will find it!

The famous Kerryman Jackie Healy-Rae put his foot in it at a time when the tourist industry in Kerry was going through a major slump and Killarney in particular was getting an awful drubbing. To lift the gloom, someone suggested that they put gondolas on the lakes of Killarney. Jackie's retort was: 'Who's going to feed the gondolas?'

A certain Cork county councillor made it on to *What It Says in Parliament* on BBC radio two weeks in a row – at the time a unique feat. His first quotation came at a meeting of the West Cork Roads Committee when he was asked: 'Who shall be chairman?'

He replied: 'The chair should rotovate.'

The following week at the West Cork Graves Committee he was asked: 'How deep should the graves be?'

He replied: 'Deep graves are a death trap.'

As the following collection reflects, political quotes can put down the pompous and the pretentious and just as memorably showcase the innocent blunderer:

In politics stupidity is not a handicap.

Napoleon Bonaparte

An honest politician is one who, when bought, stays bought.

Humorist Simon Cameron

Winston Churchill never spares himself in conversation. He gives himself so generously that hardly anybody else is permitted to give anything in his presence.

Aneurin Bevan

Men occasionally stumble over the truth, but most of them pick themselves up and hurry off as if nothing had happened.

Winston Churchill

A committee is a cul-de-sac into which ideas are lured and then quietly strangled.

Barnett Cocks

Merlyn Rees [former Secretary of State for Northern Ireland] wrestled with his conscience and the result was a draw.

Paddy Devlin (attributed)

There was no sex in Ireland before television.

Oliver J. Flanagan (attributed)

It's a good idea; somebody ought to start it.

Mahatma Gandhi, when questioned on what he thought about Western civilisation.

A committee is a group of the unwilling, picked from the unfit, to do the unnecessary.

Richard Harkness

It's sheer murder in the office every morning.

State Pathologist John Harbison, as reported in The Irish Sun *in July 2003.*

I have no interest in sailing round the world. Not that there is any lack of requests for me to do so.

Edward Heath

I don't know what people have got against the government – they've done nothing.

Bob Hope

It's very nice, you feel like you've been able to leave something behind.
Gloria Hunniford, on a visit to the toilets of Buckingham Palace.

If the word 'No' was removed from the English language, Ian Paisley would be speechless.

John Hume

Anyone who is capable of getting themselves made President should on no account be allowed to do the job.

Douglas Adams

Outside of the killings, Washington has one of the lowest crime rates in the country.
Washington, D.C., Mayor Marion Barry

If you give Congress a chance to vote on both sides of an issue, it will always do it.

Les Aspin

I don't want to sound like I have made no mistakes. I'm confident I have. I just haven't.
President George Bush, speaking in April 2004 when he was asked what was his biggest mistake after 9/11.

Sometimes I look at Billy and Jimmy and I say to myself, 'Lillian, you should have stayed a virgin'.
Lillian Carter, mother of former US President Jimmy Carter.

Congressmen have been bought and sold so many times they should have bar codes.

Contemporary Comedy magazine

If George Bush was drowning, his whole life would pass in front of him and he wouldn't be in it.

Clive James

Sure, let him join our campaign. I'd prefer to have him inside our tent pissing out, than outside our tent pissing in.

Lyndon Johnson

The secret service is under orders that if Bush is shot, to shoot Quayle.

John Kerry, talking about George Bush Sr.

The main difference for the history of the world if I had been shot rather than Kennedy, is that Onassis probably wouldn't have married Mrs Khrushchev.

Nikita Khrushchev

Apart from that Mrs Lincoln, how did you enjoy the play?

Tom Lehrer

A year ago, Gerald Ford was unknown throughout America. Now he's unknown throughout the world.

Norman Mailer

Democracy is a pathetic belief in the collective wisdom of individual ignorance.

H.L. Mencken

I am thoroughly in favour of Mrs Thatcher's visit to the Falklands. I find a bit of hesitation, though, about her coming back.

John Mortimer

Actually, I vote Labour – but my butler's Tory.

Louis Mountbatten

Politicians are wedded to the truth, but like many other married couples they sometimes live apart.

H.H. Munro

The voters have spoken – the bastards.

Richard Nixon

Former President Carter said that Bill Clinton brought disgrace to the White House with his last-minute pardon of Marc Rich. After hearing this, President Clinton denied the accusation and said that was not how he brought disgrace to the White House.

US talk-show host Conan O'Brien

I want to tell you about the Co-operative Movement. You'll get f*** all co-operation.

The greeting a Co-op leader gave to Tony O'Reilly on his first day as head of the Milk Marketing Board.

I am sorry that I cannot address the people of Latin America in their own language, which is Latin.

Dan Quayle

If you had to write an autobiography, who would it be about?

Dan Quayle to George Bush Sr

When I die, I want to be buried in Chicago so I can still be active in politics.

Representative Charlie Rangel

I never drink coffee at lunch – I find it keeps me awake for the afternoon.

Ronald Reagan

I have orders to be awakened at any time in case of a national emergency, even if I'm in a cabinet meeting.

Ronald Reagan

You'll notice that Nancy Reagan never drinks water when Ronnie speaks.

Robin Williams

De Valera discloses the workings of a mind to which incoherence lends an illusion of profundity.

T. De Vere White

We want to dehumanise the social welfare system.

Albert Reynolds

As long as I am Taoiseach, I will strive to bring employment down and, you can take it from me, that is government policy.

Albert Reynolds

Princes Charles's ears are so big, he could hang-glide across the Falklands.

Joan Rivers

As we know, there are known knowns; these are things we know we know. We also know there are unknown unknowns; that is to say we know there are some things we do not know. But there are also unknown unknowns – the ones we don't know we don't know.

Donald Rumsfeld, United States Secretary of Defence.

Ronald Reagan won because he ran against Jimmy Carter. If he had run unopposed he would have lost.

Mort Sahl

As for the look on Dan Quayle's face – how to describe it? If a tree fell in a forest, and no one was there to hear it, it might sound like Dan Quayle looks.

Tom Shales

The right honourable gentleman is indebted to his memory for his jests, and to his imagination for his facts.

Richard Brinsley Sheridan

I don't know what I would do without Whitelaw. Everyone should have a Willy.

Margaret Thatcher, talking about William Whitelaw

I am extraordinarily patient, provided I get my own way in the end.

Margaret Thatcher

Suppose you were an idiot. And suppose you were a member of Congress. But I repeat myself.

Mark Twain

He [a neighbour] stood twice for parliament, but so diffidently that his candidature passed almost unnoticed.

Evelyn Waugh

Harold Wilson is going around the country stirring up apathy.

William Whitelaw

Chapter 16 Mr President

George Bernard Shaw rather caustically defined a newspaper as a device 'unable to distinguish between a bicycle accident and the collapse of civilisation'. Hence it is no surprise that the media had a field-day with the career of Bill Clinton. There is no political agenda in this book. I have simply followed the 'joke trail'. For example, you may be surprised to find that are more jokes about Bill and Hillary Clinton than George Bush. This is not because I prefer Dubya, but simply because, at the moment, there are more jokes in circulation about the Clintons. Mind you, Bush is catching up quickly!

This chapter aims to entertain rather than to educate, focussing as it does on Clinton's less glorious episodes rather than his contribution to the Northern Ireland and Middle East peace processes. Few politicians throughout history have generated the same amount of passion as Clinton. The following stories indicate why.

Young love

President and Mrs Clinton were holidaying in their home state of Arkansas. One day they went on a trip and stopped at a service station to fill up the car with petrol. To their surprise, the station was owned by Hillary's high school boyfriend. They exchanged hellos and went on their way.

As they were driving on to their destination, Bill put his arm around Hillary and said, 'Well, honey, if you had stayed with him, you would be the wife of a service station owner today'.

She smirked and replied, 'No, if I had stayed with him, he would be President of the United States'.

Unresolved questions

During his visit to the United States, the late Pope John Paul II met with President Clinton. Instead of just an hour, as scheduled, the meeting went on for two days. Finally, a weary President Clinton emerged to face the waiting media. The President announced that the summit was a resounding success. He said that he and the Pope had agreed on 80 per cent of the matters they discussed. Then Clinton declared he was going home to the White House to be with his family.

A few minutes later, the Pope came out to make his statement. He looked tired, discouraged and practically in tears. Sadly, he announced that his meeting with the President had been a failure.

Incredulous, one reporter asked, 'But your Holiness, President Clinton just announced that the summit was a great success and the two of you agreed on 80 per cent of the items discussed.'

Exasperated, the Pope answered, 'Yes, but we were talking about the 10 Commandments.'

In the soup

At the height of the Lewinsky scandal Campbell's announced they would be stocking America's shelves with a new product called 'Clinton soup'. Named after a distinguished politician, it consisted of one small weenie in hot water.

Briefs

Q: Why does Bill Clinton wear boxers?
A: To keep his ankles warm.
Q: What did they find in Monica Lewinsky's dress pocket?
A: A wad of bills.

Library service

Future historians will be able to study and do research at:
• The John F. Kennedy Presidential Library.
• The Lyndon B. Johnson Presidential Library.
• The Richard M. Nixon Presidential Library.

- The Gerald M. Ford Presidential Library.
- The Ronald Reagan Presidential Library.
- The George Bush Sr Presidential Library

And…

- The William J. Clinton Adult Bookstore.

Computer

In 1999, two young female White House interns met for lunch at a restaurant. One girl said, 'Hey, I just heard that the White House got a new computer.'

The other girl said, 'Really? What kind?'

The first girl said, 'All I know is, it's got a big hard drive and no memory.'

The 12th of never

After the White House sex scandal, 500 women were asked if they would sleep with President Clinton.

- 20% said no.
- 15% said maybe.
- 65% said never again.

If only

In an interview, Pamela Anderson said that if she were Hillary, she would leave President Clinton. In response, Clinton said, 'If Pamela Anderson were Hillary, none of this would have happened in the first place'.

Right on

Bill Clinton confessed that, after the Lewinsky scandal broke, he didn't speak to his wife for six months. He didn't want to interrupt her.

When he reached rock bottom, Bill went for a long drive. He walked into a diner in a small town. The waiter came and asked him for his order. Feeling lonely, the President replied, 'Meat loaf and a kind word'.

When the waiter returned with the meat loaf, Clinton asked, 'Where's the good word?'

The waiter sighed, bent down and whispered, 'Don't eat the meat loaf'.

Situation vacant

Clinton was interviewing an attractive young woman for a White House internship. Looking over the application, he noticed that the girl had not answered one important question concerning transportation to and from work.

'What about your bus line?' Bill asked her.

'I don't believe I mentioned it,' came the pleased reply, 'but it's a 36C.'

Quote, unquote

On the first day of the school year a new student, Toshiba, who was the son of a Japanese businessman, entered the fifth grade. The teacher greeted the class and said, 'Let's begin by reviewing some American history. Who said, "Give me liberty, or give me death"? The teacher saw only a sea of blank faces, except for that of Toshiba, who had his hand up.

'Patrick Henry, 1775,' said the boy.

'Now,' continued the teacher, 'who said "Government of the people, by the people, for the people shall not perish from the Earth"?'

Again, no response except from Toshiba: 'Abraham Lincoln, 1863.'

The teacher snapped at the class, 'You should all be ashamed. Toshiba, who is new to our country, knows more about it than you do.'

Completely disgusted by Toshiba's classroom superiority, a student in the back sighed, 'I'm gonna throw up.'

'Who said that?' the teacher asked.

Again, Toshiba raised his hand and said: 'George Bush Sr to the Japanese Prime Minister, 1991.'

Now furious, another student yelled, 'Oh yeah, well suck my ****
[a word denoting a man's private organs]'. Once again it was Toshiba with the answer, 'Bill Clinton to Monica Lewinsky, 1997.'

Clinton's legacy

While President, Clinton revised the judicial oath: 'I solemnly swear to tell the truth as I know it, the whole truth as I know it, the whole truth as I believe it to be, and nothing but what I think you need to know.'

Parallel lines

Not a lot of people know this, but there are many similarities between the tragic story in the film *Titanic* and the life and times of Bill Clinton. Need evidence? Consider the following:

Titanic: Jack is a starving artist.

Clinton: Bill is a bulls*** artist.

Titanic: In one scene, Jack enjoys a good cigar.

Clinton: Ditto for Bill.

Titanic: During the ordeal, Rose's dress gets ruined.

Clinton: Ditto for Monica.

Titanic: Rose remembers Jack for the rest of her life.

Clinton: Clinton doesn't remember jack.

Titanic: Rose goes down on a vessel full of seamen.

Clinton: Monica…ooh, let's not go there.

Titanic: Jack surrenders to an icy death.

Clinton: Bill goes home to Hillary – basically the same thing.

Rest in peace

Bill Clinton died and went to heaven. When St Peter greeted him at the Pearly Gates, Bill asked if he would be allowed into God's kingdom.

'Sure,' said the saint. 'But first you have to confess your sins. What bad things have you done in your life?'

Clinton bit his lip and answered, 'Well, I tried marijuana, but you can't call it dope-smoking because I didn't inhale. There were inappropriate extramarital relationships – but you can't call it adultery because I didn't have full "sexual relations". And I made some statements that were misleading but legally accurate – you can't call it bearing false witness because, as far as I know, it didn't meet the legal standard of perjury.'

With that St Peter consulted the Book of Life and declared, 'OK, here's the deal. We'll send you somewhere hot, but we won't call it "hell". You'll be there indefinitely, but we won't call it eternity. And then when you enter you don't have to "abandon all hope", just don't hold your breath waiting for it to freeze over.'

Fatherly chat

Bill Clinton: 'Chelsea, come in here, we need to talk.'

Chelsea: 'What's up, Dad?'

Bill: 'There's a scratch down the side of the car. Did you do it?'

Chelsea: 'I don't believe, if I understand the definition of "scratch on the car", that I can say, truthfully, that I scratched the car.'

Bill: 'Well, it wasn't there yesterday, and you drove the car last night, and no one else has driven it since. How can you explain the scratch?'

Chelsea: 'Well, as I've said before, I have no recollection of scratching the car. While it is true that I did take the car out last night, *I* did not scratch it.'

Bill: 'But someone has told me she saw you back the car against the mailbox at the end of the driveway, heard a loud scraping noise, saw you get out examine the car, and then drive away. So again, I'll ask you, yes or no, did you scratch the car?'

Chelsea: 'Oh, you mean you think you have evidence to prove I scratched it. Well, you see, I understood you to mean did "I" scratch the car. I stand by my earlier statement, that "I" did not scratch the car.'

Bill: 'Are you trying to tell me you didn't drive the car into the mailbox?'

Chelsea: 'Well, you see, Sir, I was trying to drive the car into the street. I mishandled the steering of the car, and it resulted in direct contact with the mailbox, though that was clearly not my intent.'

Bill: 'So, you are then saying that you did hit the mailbox?'

Chelsea: 'No Sir, that's not my statement. I'll refer you back to my original statement that I did not scratch the car.'

Bill: 'But the car did hit the mailbox, and the car did get scratched as a result of this contact?'

Chelsea: 'Well, yes, I suppose you could look at it that way.'

Bill: 'So you lied to me when you said you did not scratch the car?'

Chelsea: 'No, that's not correct. Your question was "Did I scratch the car?" From a strictly legal definition, as I understood the meaning of that sentence, "I" did not scratch the car…the mailbox did…I was merely present when the scratching occurred. So my answer of "No" when you asked whether I scratched the car was legally correct, although I did not volunteer that information.'

Bill: 'Where did you learn to be such a smart ass?'

Chelsea: 'From you, Dad.'

Daddy's girl

Hillary Clinton was having a heart-to-heart talk with her daughter, Chelsea, and asked, 'Have you had sex yet?'

Chelsea replied, 'Not according to Dad.'

Snow secrets

When he was President, Bill Clinton stepped out onto the White House lawn in the dead of winter. Right in front of him, he saw 'The President Must Die' written in urine across the snow. Bill was furious. He stormed into the Secret Service compound and yelled: 'There's a death threat on the front lawn and it's written in urine. I want to know who did it, and I want to know NOW.'

The Secret Service agents scurried for the door. That evening, the chief agent approached Clinton and said, 'Mr President, we have some bad news and some really bad news. Which do you want first?'

Bill replied, 'Give me the bad news first.'

The agent said, 'Sir, we tested a sample of the urine. The results just come back. The urine belongs to Al Gore.'

'Oh my God. I feel so betrayed. My Vice President. What's the "really" bad news?'

'Sir, the handwriting belongs to Hillary.'

Trivial pursuit

After much arguing and deliberation, historians this week have come up with a phrase to describe the Clinton era. It will be called: SEX BETWEEN THE BUSHES.

The Centre for Disease control in Atlanta announced that Clinton has proven that you can get sex from Aides.

Jennifer Flowers was asked if her relationship with Clinton was anything like Monica Lewinsky's. She replied, 'Close but no cigar.'

The FBI has coined a technical term for the stains found on Monica's dress: 'Presidue.'

Clinton now recruits interns from only four colleges: Moorhead, Oral Roberts, Ball State and Brigham Young.

Clinton once asked that the Democratic Party emblem be changed to a condom. It represents inflation, halts production and gives you a sense of security when you are being screwed.

Every breath you take

After Monicagate, Hillary took to trailing Bill everywhere he went. A piece of graffiti appeared on the wall in the men's room of the President's favourite bar: 'My wife follows me everywhere.'

Written just below it was: 'I do not.'

Good advice

When she was First Lady, Hillary Clinton was having a woman-to-woman talk with the Attorney General, Janet Reno. 'You're lucky that you don't have to have sex with men. I have to put up with Bill, and there is no telling where he last had his pecker.'

Janet responded, 'Just because journalists say I am not pretty doesn't mean I don't have to fight off unwelcome sexual advances.'

Hillary asked, 'Well, how do you deal with this problem?'

Janet said, 'Whenever I feel that a guy is getting ready to make a pass at me, I muster all my might and squeeze out the loudest, nastiest fart that I can.'

That night, Bill was already asleep with the lights out when Hillary slipped into bed. She could hear him start to stir, and knew that he would want some action. She had been saving her 'wind' all day, and let out a disgusting sound.

Bill rolled over and said, 'Janet, is that you?'

Generous gestures

Janet Reno inserted an advert in the classifieds: 'Husband wanted.' The next day she received 100 letters. They all said the same thing: 'You can have mine.'

Possession is nine-tenths of the law

Hillary woke Bill at 3 am to tell him she had to go to the bathroom. He asked her: 'Why are you waking me to tell me that?'

She said, 'I want you to save my place.'

The Wizard of Oz

Dan Quayle, George Bush Sr and Bill Clinton were riding in a car in the Midwest when they were caught in a tornado. The car was thrown into the sky. When it landed, the politicians found themselves in the Land of Oz.

'I'm going to see the Wizard and ask him to give me a brain,' said Quayle.

'I'm going to ask the Wizard to give me a heart,' said Bush.

'Where's Dorothy?' asked Clinton.

When a child is born

In 1999, Hillary Clinton went to her doctor because she was not feeling well. The doctor explained that she was pregnant again. Hillary was furious, as having another child would ruin her plans to run for the New York Senate. The more she thought about it, the madder she got. She was so mad that she called Bill at the Oval Office and began to scream at him, telling him that he had selfishly gotten her pregnant and ruined her dreams of running for the Senate. She went on and on. Finally there was a long pause as she waited for a reply from Mr Clinton. Suddenly, after the long silence, Bill said, 'Who is this?'

Statesmanlike

Six statesmen are on a sinking boat.

Tony Blair asks: 'What do we do?'

Nelson Mandela says: 'Man the lifeboats.'

Ronald Reagan says: 'What lifeboats?'

Mahatma Gandhi says: 'Women first.'

George Bush says: 'Screw the women.'

Bill Clinton says: 'You think we have the time?'

Affairs of the heart

Have you heard about this young boy called Bill, who could think about nothing but girls, girls and more girls? However, he has outgrown it. Now all he thinks about are women.

Love affairs

Chelsea Clinton went off to college and met this really handsome guy named John. They started dating and pretty soon John asked Chelsea to marry him and she said 'Yes'. Chelsea was so excited that she called her dad to tell him the great news.

As soon as Bill found out who she was going to marry he said, 'I'm sorry, honey, but you can't marry him.'

'Why not?'

'Well, you see this is the way it is. Many years ago I had an affair with John's mother and John is actually my illegitimate son, so you can't marry him.'

Chelsea was heartbroken. She told John that she wouldn't marry him and was very depressed until she met James. They dated for a while and soon James asked her to marry him. Again, Chelsea ran to the phone to tell her father the great news. As soon as Bill heard who his daughter wanted to marry he said, 'I'm sorry, honey, but you can't marry him either.'

'Why not?'

'For the same reason. James is my illegitimate son.'

Chelsea was again very heartbroken.

However, one day she met this really nice guy named Jack. Jack asked Chelsea out. Before she agreed to go out with him, Chelsea called her dad and asked him whether she and Jack were related.

'I'm sorry to tell you this honey, but Jack is also your brother.'

At this point Chelsea was getting really ticked off, so she called her mother to complain. 'Every guy who asks me out turns out to be Daddy's illegitimate son.'

'Oh, don't worry about that,' said Hillary.

'Why not?' asked Chelsea.

'Because Bill Clinton is not really your father.'

Why did the chicken cross the road?

Pat Buchanan: 'To steal a job from a decent, hardworking American.'

Colonel Sanders: 'I missed one?'

L.A. Police Department: 'Give us five minutes with the chicken and we'll find out.'

Bill Clinton: 'The chicken did not cross the road. I repeat, the chicken did not cross the road. I don't know any chickens. I have never known any chickens.'

Martin Luther King Jr: 'I envision a world where all chickens will be free to cross roads without having their motives called into question.'

Grandpa: 'In my day, we didn't ask why the chicken crossed the road. Someone told us that the chicken crossed the road, and that was good enough for us.'

Karl Marx: 'It was an historical inevitability.'

Saddam Hussein: 'This was an unprovoked act of rebellion and we were quite justified in dropping 50 tons of nerve gas on the chicken.'

Bill Clinton (again): 'I did not cross the road with THAT chicken. However, I did ask a friend to find the chicken a job in Washington.'

Captain James T. Kirk: 'To boldly go where no chicken has gone before.'

Machiavelli: 'The point is that the chicken crossed the road. Who cares why? The end of crossing the road justifies whatever motive there was.'

Freud: 'The fact that you are at all concerned that the chicken crossed the road reveals your underlying sexual insecurity.'

Bill Gates: 'I have just released "Chicken Coop 2005", which will not only cross roads, but will lay eggs, file your important documents and balance your chequebook. Explorer is an inextricable part of the operating system.'

Einstein: 'Did the chicken really cross the road or did the road move beneath the chicken?'

Bill Clinton (also, again): 'Define "cross".'

Time

One day Hillary Clinton was struck by a car and killed. Hillary found herself at the gates of heaven. She saw St Peter and asked, 'Can I get into heaven now?' He said, 'Soon, I have some things to take care of.' So St Peter left and Hillary looked at the scenery and saw millions of clocks lying around. Every once in a while, a clock or so would turn ahead 15 minutes. Hillary wondered why.

St Peter came back and Hillary asked, 'St Peter, what are all the clocks for?'

St Peter replied, 'Each clock represents a man. Every time a man commits adultery, the clock turns ahead 15 minutes.'

Hillary asked, 'Where's my husband's clock?'

St Peter replied, 'Oh, it's in God's office, he uses it as a fan.'

A parable

Bill Clinton told the story of a father who always tucked his daughter, Sarah, into bed. Every night she knelt down and said her prayers. One night, she prayed: 'Please God, I want to thank you for giving me Mommy, Daddy and Grandpa. I want you to especially look after Grandma tomorrow.' The next day Sarah's grandmother was killed in a car crash.

That night Sarah's dad listened as she said her prayers: 'Please God, I want to thank you for giving me Mommy and Daddy. I want you to especially look after Grandpa tomorrow.' The next day there was a storm and Sarah's grandfather was killed by a falling tree.

That night, Sarah's dad listened with even keener interest than normal as his daughter said her prayers. 'Please God, I want to thank you for giving me Mommy. I want you to especially look after my father tomorrow.'

The next day Sarah's dad drove more carefully to work than ever before. He refused to leave the office all day and drove home from work so slowly that a cyclist overtook him. When he got home safely he breathed a sigh of relief and had a few quick drinks. As the relief flooded over him he turned to his wife and asked her how her day was. She replied: 'Oh, it was terrible. It was the worst day ever. My very good friend, Pat the mailman, collapsed at the foot of our stairs this morning and died of a heart attack.'

Fantasy

One night, Bill and Hillary were lying in bed when he noticed that she had bought a new book entitled *What 20 Million American Women Want.*

Bill grabbed the book out of her hands and started thumbing through the pages. Hillary was a little annoyed, 'Hey, what do you think you're doing?'

Bill calmly replied, 'I just wanted to see if they spelled my name right.'

What women want

One day, a woman Bill Clinton had had an affair with was walking along the beach, when she found a bottle in the sand. When she opened the bottle, a genie appeared in front of her. 'I'll grant you three wishes for freeing me, but beware as, whatever you wish for, your ex-love will get twice as much.'

'But that rat left me for another,' replied the woman.

'I'm sorry, but that's what it says in the rule book,' said the genie.

'All right. First I want a $1 million,' and at her feet the money appeared. However, miles away $2 million was put at Clinton's feet.

'Secondly, I want a diamond necklace.' At her feet was a beautiful necklace and immediately there were two necklaces at Clinton's feet.

'And thirdly, please scare me half to death.'

Celluloid exploits

Liberals will be shocked to learn that Clinton strongly objects to sex in the cinema: 'I hate sex in the movies. Tried it once, the seat folded up, the drink spilled and that ice, well it really chilled her mood.'

Confusion

One night, while he was in college in Oxford, Bill Clinton was out having a good time. His bored roommate was in the room alone when the phone rang. A young woman's voice came over the line. 'Can I speak to Bill, please?'

'I'm sorry, he's not in right now. Can I take a message?'

'Do you know what time he'll be back?'

'I think he said he'd be home around 10.'

Awkward silence.

'Do you want to leave a message for Bill? I'll be happy to pass it on to him as soon as he comes in.'

'Well...he said he would be in at this time and asked me to call him.'

'Well, he went out with Rennie about an hour ago and said he would be back at 10.'

A shocked voice now: 'Who the fu...who is Rennie?'

'The girl he went out with.'

'I know that! I mean...who the fu...who is she?'

'I don't know her last name. Look, do you want to leave a message for Bill?'

'Yes...please do. Tell him to call me when he gets in.'

'I sure will. Is this Mary-Kate?'

'Who the f****** hell is Mary-Kate?'

'Well, he's going out with Mary-Kate at 10. I thought you were her. Sorry. It was an honest mistake.'

'Bill's the one who made the mistake! Tell him that Liz called and that's she's very upset and that I would like him to call me as soon as he gets in.'

'Okay, I will…but Samantha isn't going to like this.'

The phone was slammed down with venom.

A lucky catch?

Last week Bill Clinton went into a seafood restaurant and pulled a mussel.

Riddle me this

Q: What is Bill Clinton's favourite band?

A: Cheap Trick.

Q: What is unusual about the new Bill Clinton Commemorative Holiday Belt Buckle?

A: It is made out of mistletoe.

Q: Bill Clinton, what do you think of Foreign Affairs?

A: I don't know. I've never had one.

Q: Why are they planning to bury Bill Clinton 12 feet under at his funeral?

A: Because deep down he's a really good person.

The heckler

When Bill Clinton gave a major address in New Jersey, he was loudly heckled by a woman in the crowd. She screamed at him, calling him 'a draft-dodging lying womaniser'.

Clinton's response to her was, 'Well, hey! You married me.'

For sale

After he got married, Bill Clinton took out an ad in the local paper. It read as follows: 'For sale by owner: Complete set of *Encyclopaedia Britannica*. No longer needed – wife knows everything.'

Born to run

Since his recent health scares Bill Clinton has gone for a jog every morning. Every day on his normal route, he passed a prostitute on a street corner. Every day she shouted out, 'You can have me for $50.'

Bill always replied, '$5.'

One day Hillary decided that she wanted to accompany her husband on his jog. As the jogging couple neared the problematic street corner, Bill knew that the 'pro' would bark her $50 offer. Hillary would then wonder what he'd really been doing on all his past outings. The former President knew that he should have a darn good explanation for the Senator.

As they jogged into the turn that would take them past the corner, Bill became very apprehensive. Sure enough, there was the prostitute. Bill tried to avoid her eyes as she watched the pair jog past.

Then, from the sidewalk, the prostitute yelled, 'See what you get for five bucks.'

In the genes

The young Chelsea Clinton went up to her father and asked: 'Dad, where did all of my intelligence come from?'

Bill replied, 'Well love, you must have got it from your mother, cause I still have mine.'

Looks can be deceiving

A doctor examined Hillary Clinton, took Bill aside, and said, 'I don't like the look of your wife at all.'

Bill replied, 'Me neither, doc. But she's a great cook and really good with our daughter.'

Cursed

Bill Clinton went to a wizard to ask him if he could remove a curse he had been living with for years. The wizard replied, 'Maybe, but you will have to tell me the exact words that were used to put the curse on you.'

Bill said without hesitation, 'I now pronounce you man and wife.'

Tight fit

Not a lot of people know this but Bill Clinton first met Hillary at a bar where she was wearing the tightest trousers he'd ever seen. At the time his curiosity got the better of him, so he walked over and asked her, 'How do you get into those pants?' She looked at him and said, 'Well, you could start by buying me a drink.'

I gave you the best years of my life

On an airplane a stewardess, who was about to get married, was delighted to hear that it was the Clintons' wedding anniversary. She congratulated them and asked how they had stayed together for so long.

'It has all felt like five minutes…' Bill said slowly.

The stewardess was just about to remark on how sweet that was when Bill finished his sentence with a word that earned him a sharp smack on the head from Hillary:

'…underwater.'

A wedding vow

The night of their wedding, Bill put a box under the marital bed and told Hillary that she must never open it. Hillary solemnly agreed to this. For 25 years she was faithful to that promise, but on their 25th anniversary she yielded to temptation and examined the contents of the box.

That evening they went out for a special anniversary dinner. After the meal, Hillary could no longer contain her curiosity and confessed: 'I'm so sorry. But now I need to know, why do you keep the three empty beer cans in the box?'

Bill thought for a while and said, 'I guess after all these years you deserve to know the truth. Whenever I was unfaithful to you, I put an empty beer can in the box under the bed to remind myself not to do it again.'

Hillary was shocked but said, 'Hmmmm, Jennifer, Paula and Monica. I am very saddened and disappointed by your behaviour. However, since you are so addicted to sex, I guess it does happen and I suppose three times is not that bad considering your problem.'

Bill thanked her for being so understanding. They hugged and made their peace. A little while later, Hillary asked, 'So why do you have all that money in the box?'

Bill answered, 'Well, whenever the box filled up with empty cans, I took them to the recycling centre and redeemed them for cash.'

On the up

One of Bill Clinton's favourite stories, for obvious reasons, is about an Amish boy and his father who visited a shopping mall. They were amazed by almost everything they saw, but especially by two shiny, silver walls that could move apart and back together again. The boy asked: 'What is this?' The father (never having seen a lift) responded, 'Son, I have never seen anything like this in my life. I don't know what it is.'

While the boy and his father were watching wide-eyed, an old lady in a wheelchair rolled up to the moving walls and pressed a button. The walls opened and the lady rolled between them into a small room. The walls closed and the boy and his father watched small circles above the walls light up. They continued to watch the circles light up in the reverse direction. The walls opened up again and a beautiful 25-year-old woman stepped out. The father said to his son, 'Go get your mother.'

Horse sense

Bill Clinton was sitting reading his newspaper when Hillary sneaked up behind him and whacked him on the head with a frying pan.

'What was that for?' he asked. 'That was for the piece of paper in your trouser pocket with the name of Mary Ellen written on it,' his wife replied.

'Don't be silly,' the former President explained. 'Two weeks ago when I went to the races, Mary Ellen was the name of one of the horses I bet on.'

This seemed to satisfy Hillary and she apologised. Three days later, he was sitting in his chair reading when she nailed him with an even bigger frying pan, knocking him out cold. When he came around he asked, 'What was that for?'

His wife said, 'Your horse phoned.'

Dear Sir or Madam

The following letter has been recently circulating in the Democratic Party circles.

```
Dear Friend:

    We have the distinguished honour of being on the
committee to raise $5 million for the monument of
Bill Clinton. We originally wanted to put him on
Mount Rushmore, until we saw that there was not
enough room for two more faces.
    We then decided to erect a statue of Bill Clinton
in the Washington, DC, Hall of Fame. We were in a
quandary as to where the statue should be placed.
We finally decided to place it beside Christopher
Columbus, the greatest Democrat of all. He left not
knowing where he was going, did not know where he
was, returned to where he had been, and did it all
on someone else's money.
    If you are one of the fortunate people who have
anything left after taxes, we expect a generous
contribution to this worthwhile project.

    Thank you,
    Bill Clinton Monument Committee

    PS The committee has raised over $1.35 so far.
```

Rabbiting on

After Bill Clinton left the White House he struggled to find a weekend apartment, as the housing market in America was as tight as ours in Dublin. After searching for months he found the perfect place. The problem was, Bill owns a dog, and the landlord specified 'No dogs'. Rather than go on searching, the former President decided not to tell the landlord about his dog (a golden retriever).

All went well for a few months. Except for one thing. The family that lived downstairs had a rabbit that they kept in a cage in the garden area. One day, the father of the family walked into the garden to find the dog scratching at the cage, trying to get at the rabbit.

He immediately went to the landlord and complained. The landlord threatened to kick Bill out. But Clinton, who was quite persuasive and punctual with rent cheques, convinced the landlord to keep him and his dog, on condition that Bill kept his dog out of the garden.

Months went by without incident. However, one day Chelsea stayed over at his place. Not knowing the garden rule, she let the dog out. Bill came home and, to his dismay, found that his dog wasn't in the house. He opened the back door, and there at the steps was his dog, dead rabbit in mouth. Needless to say, Bill panicked. Not wanting to face certain eviction and possible jail time, he took matters into his own hands.

He bathed the dead rabbit, blow-dried its hair (OK, he was desperate) and carefully placed the rabbit back in the cage. Natural causes, right?

Nothing happened. After an excruciating week, he finally approached his neighbour. 'How is everything?' asked Bill.

'We're moving,' replied the man. 'This is a sick neighbourhood.'

'Why? What happened?' queried Bill.

The neighbour answered, 'Some sick person dug up our recently deceased rabbit, washed it, combed its hair and put it back in its cage.'

You're in the army now

One Sunday, Bill Clinton came out of church. As always, the preacher was standing at the door shaking hands as the congregation departed. He grabbed Bill by the hand and pulled him aside.

The preacher said to him, 'You need to join the Army of the Lord.'

Clinton replied, 'I'm already in the Army of the Lord, Preacher.'

The preacher questioned, 'How come I don't see you except for Christmas and Easter?'

He whispered back, 'I'm in the secret service.'

On the house

One day, Bill came home early from the West Wing and found his Security Chief kissing Chelsea. He shouted at him, 'Is this what I pay you for?'

The Security Chief replied: 'No, Mr President, this I do free of charge.'

A pig's dinner

President Clinton returned from holiday. He walked down the steps of Air Force One with two pigs under his arms. As he reached the bottom of the steps, the guardsman stepped forward and remarked, 'Nice pigs, Mr President'.

The President replied, 'I'll have you know that these are genuine Arkansas razorback hogs. I got this one for Chelsea and this one for Hillary…So, now what do you think?'

The guardsman answered, 'Nice trade, Sir.'

A mother's love

Clinton's mother prayed devoutly that Bill would grow up and be President of the United States. So far, half of her prayer has been answered.

Affairs of state

As US President, Bill Clinton gave new meaning to the phrase 'affairs of state'. However, there were times when his extracurricular activities switched from playing around to playing a round. At one stage, Bill got the chance to play golf with Tiger Woods. It was a particularly poor day on the greens for Clinton. His embarrassment was compounded by the fact that he was doing so badly in front of the greatest player in the world. He said to Tiger, 'I'd move heaven and earth to play like you.'

Tiger very apologetically said, 'Thank you, Mr President. If I were you, though, I'd concentrate just on heaven. You've moved enough earth today.'

A discerning eye

Taking advantage of a balmy day in New York, Bill Clinton donned his polo shirt and khakis for a game of golf. Before he teed off, he watched four men produce some really horrible shots. After 20 minutes watching the foursome Bill asked, 'You guys wouldn't be priests by any chance?'

'Actually, yes, we are,' one cleric replied. 'How did you know?'

'Easy. I've never seen such bad golf and such clean language.'

Foreplay

On a very crowded golf course in Washington DC, four women teed off. There were four politicians ahead of them. One of the women hit the ball like a bullet and before she could shout 'Fore', it hit Bill Clinton. He fell to the ground holding his crotch. The ladies were embarrassed, but after they regained their composure one of the women said, 'I'm a physiotherapist and I will deal with the problem. Would everyone please leave me alone with this poor man for a few minutes.' Everybody moved away. At first Bill refused to let her touch him, but eventually he yielded to her feminine charms. She opened his trousers and massaged him gently on the crotch area for five minutes until finally she stopped.

She tenderly asked, 'How does that feel?'

Clinton replied, 'It feels terrific but my thumb is still killing me!'

On the bill

Bill's enthusiasm for the game of golf is not matched by his talent. Once, one of his drives landed on an anthill. Rather than move the ball, Bill decided to hit it where it lay. He gave a mighty swing. Clouds of dirt, sand and ants exploded from the spot – everything, that is, but the golf ball. Bill lined up and tried another shot. Again, clouds of dirt, sand and ants went flying, but the golf ball didn't even wiggle. Two ants survived. One dazed ant said to the other, 'What are we going to do?' The other replied, 'I don't know about you, but I'm going to get on the ball.'

A simple misunderstanding

Bill and Hillary Clinton were at a Yankees game. Before the game started a Secret Service agent came up to Bill and whispered in his ear. Bill suddenly picked up Hillary and threw her out on the field.

The Secret Service man came running up to him and said, 'Mr President, Sir, I think you misunderstood me; I said they want you to throw out the first pitch.'

Getting your teeth into it

Bill and Hillary walked into a dentist's office. Bill said to the dentist, 'Doc, I'm in one hell of a big hurry. I have two buddies sitting in the car waiting for us to play golf. So, forget about the anaesthetic and just pull the tooth and be done with it. I don't have time to wait for the anaesthetic to work.'

The dentist thought to himself, 'My goodness, Clinton is a very brave man, asking me to pull his tooth without using anything to kill the pain.'

So the dentist asked him, 'Which tooth is it, Mr President?'

Bill turned to Hillary and said, 'Open your mouth, honey, and show the doctor which tooth hurts.'

Mr right and wrong

At a cocktail party, a woman said to Hillary, 'Aren't you wearing your wedding ring on the wrong finger?'

'Yes, I am,' she replied. 'I married the wrong man.'

Husbands and wives

When Hillary Clinton became pregnant, she dragged Bill to a maternity class. All the fathers were told to wear a bag of sand to give them an idea of what it felt like to be pregnant. Bill stood up and shrugged saying, 'This doesn't feel so bad'.

The instructor then dropped a pen and asked the husband to pick it up. 'You want me to pick up the pen as if I were pregnant, the way my wife would do it?' Bill asked.

'Exactly,' replied the instructor.

To the delight of the other husbands, he turned to Hillary and said, 'Honey, pick up that pen for me'.

The old cow

Hillary Clinton's chauffeur knocked down an old cow. Hillary sent him to the farmhouse to explain what had happened, not realising that the owners were Republicans. Three hours later, he returned looking elated but carrying a bottle of wine, smoking a cigar and smeared with lipstick.

'What happened?' asked Hillary.

The driver replied, 'Well, the farmer gave me the wine, his wife gave me the cigar, and their beautiful twin daughters made mad, passionate love to me.'

'My God, what did you tell them?' asked Hillary.

The driver replied, 'I'm Hillary Clinton's driver, and I just killed the old cow.'

A dog's life

A woman was leaving a convenience store with her morning coffee when she noticed a most unusual funeral procession approaching the nearby cemetery. Two long, black hearses drove past. Hillary Clinton, with a pit bull on a leash, walked behind the second hearse. Behind her, a short distance back, were about 200 women walking in single file.

The woman was so curious that she respectfully approached Hillary and said, 'I am so sorry for your loss, and I know now is a bad time to disturb you, but I have never seen a funeral like this. Whose funeral is it?'

'My husband's.'

'What happened to him?'

Hillary replied, 'My dog attacked and killed him.'

She inquired further, 'Well, who is in the second hearse?'

Mrs Clinton answered, 'My mother-in-law. She was trying to help my husband when the dog turned on her.'

A poignant and thoughtful moment of silence passed between the two women.

'Can I borrow the dog?'

'Get in line.'

Catty

After they left the White House, Bill and Hillary moved into a more modest abode. One evening, they decided to go out to dinner. They'd gotten ready, all dolled up, cat put out, etc. The taxi arrived, and as the couple walked out, the cat shot back in. They didn't want the cat shut in the house, so Hillary went out to the taxi while Bill went upstairs to chase the cat out. Hillary, not wanting it known that the house would be empty, explained to the taxi driver: 'He's just going upstairs to say goodbye to my mother.'

A few minutes later, Bill got into the cab, 'Sorry I took so long,' he said. 'Stupid old thing was hiding under the bed and I had to poke her with a coat hanger to come out.'

Sign language

After driving up and down several lanes looking for parking at the shopping mall, a motorist finally found a spot. He noticed Bill Clinton driving very slowly in the same direction, and, since Bill was closer, the man gave him the 'Are you going to park there?' look.

Clinton's responding gestures were very confusing. First he shook his head. Next he pointed at the motorist, then at the parking space and then at himself, his watch and the mall. Finishing off, he frowned, raised his palms upward and shrugged. Once the motorist parked, he walked over to Clinton to make sure he hadn't wanted the space.

'You must be single,' Bill replied. 'If you were married, you would've known that that was the universal sign for "Go ahead and take the spot. I'm waiting for my wife".'

The juror

Bill Clinton was called for jury duty. During the jury selection process, each side hotly contested and dismissed potential jurors. Bill Clinton was called for his question session.

'Property holder?'

'Yes, I am, Your Honour.'

'Married or single?'

'Married for years, Your Honour.'

'Formed or expressed an opinion?'

'Not in many years, Your Honour.'

The marriage vows are very sacred

Bill Clinton has always been a prankster. As each of his friends got married, Bill made sure some type of practical joke was played on them. Now ready to be married himself, he was dreading the payback he knew was coming.

Surprisingly, the wedding ceremony went off without a hitch. No one stood up during the pause to offer a reason 'why this couple should not be married'. The reception wasn't disrupted by streakers or smoke bombs, and the car the couple was to take on their honeymoon was in perfect working order.

When the couple arrived at their hotel and entered the room, Bill even checked for cornflakes in the bed (a gag he had always loved). Nothing, it seemed, was amiss. Satisfied that he had come away unscathed, he took Hillary to bed. Upon waking, the couple was ravenous, so Bill called down for room service and said, 'I'd like to order breakfast for two'.

At that moment, a soft voice under the bed said, 'Make that five'.

Catch me if you can

After his health scare, Bill resolved to get fit. He signed up for a weight-loss programme that provided a personal trainer. The programme included a run each morning at 6 am. So when the doorbell rang the next morning, Bill was dressed and ready. When he opened the door, he saw the most beautiful blonde he had ever clapped eyes on. She smiled and said: 'If you can catch me, you can kiss me.' Then she ran off at a very fast pace.

This continued each morning. After about three very frustrating weeks, Bill began to get in shape and could almost catch her. One morning, he was almost able to touch her running shorts but he couldn't quite hang on to her. He thought to himself that the next day was going to be the big day. He would catch her and have her. He slept that night in eager anticipation.

The next morning, the bell rang precisely at 6 am. Bill ran to the door and threw it open. There stood a huge, burly woman, weighing over 250 pounds. She was muscled up like a plough horse. She smiled and said: 'I'm your new trainer. If I can catch you, I can kiss you.'

The first supper

One hot summer's day after the Clintons had left the White House, Bill was watching TV as Hillary was out cutting the grass. He finally worked up the energy to go out ask her what was for supper. Well, Hillary was quite irritated about him sitting in the air-conditioned house all day while she did all the work. 'I can't believe you're asking me about supper right now. Imagine I'm out of town, go inside and figure dinner out for yourself.'

So he went back in the house and fixed himself a big steak, with potatoes, garlic bread and a tall glass of iced tea. Hillary finally walked in about the time he was finishing up and asked him, 'You fixed something to eat? So where is mine?'

'Huh? I thought you were out of town.'

The Clintons on marriage

Hillary says: 'Marriages are made in heaven.'

Bill says: 'But so again, are thunder and lightning.'

Hillary says: 'Before marriage, a man will lie awake all night thinking about something you said. After marriage, he will fall asleep before you finish talking. If you want your spouse to listen and pay strict attention to every word you say, talk in your sleep.'

Bill says: 'Married life is very frustrating. In the first year of marriage, the man speaks and the woman listens. In the second year, the woman speaks and the man listens. In the third year, they both speak and the neighbours listen.'

Hillary says: 'When a man opens the door of a car for his wife, you can be sure of one thing: Either the car is new or the wife is.'

Bill says: 'Man is incomplete until he marries. After that, he is finished.'

Hillary says: 'Every woman wants a man who is handsome, understanding, economical, a good cook and a considerate lover, but the law allows only one husband.'

Bill says: 'Every man wants a wife who is beautiful, understanding, economical and a good cook. But the law allows only one wife.'

Chelsea: 'Is it true, that in some parts of the world a man doesn't know his wife until he marries her?'

Bill: 'That happens in every country.'

Hillary: 'Women will never be equal to men until they can walk down the street with a bald head and a beer gut, and still think they are attractive to the opposite sex.'

Chelsea: 'How much does a wedding cost?'

Bill: 'I don't know; I'm still paying for it.'

Hillary: 'I never knew what real happiness was until I got married, and by then, it was too late.'

Bill: 'You have two choices in life: You can stay single and be miserable, or get married and wish you were dead.'

Hillary: 'When a woman steals your husband, there is no better revenge than to let her keep him.'

The perfect husband

Several men were in the locker room of a golf club. A cellphone on a bench rang and a man engaged the hands-free speaker function and answered the call. Everyone else in the room stopped to listen.

Man: 'Hello.'

Hillary Clinton: 'Honey, it's me. Are you at the club?'

Man: 'Yes.'

Hillary: 'I'm at the mall now and I've found this beautiful leather coat. It's only $1,000. Is it ok if I buy it?'

Man: 'Sure, go ahead if you like it that much.'

Hillary: 'I also stopped by the Mercedes dealership and saw the new 2005 models. I saw one I really liked.'

Man: 'How much?'

Hillary: '$65,000.'

Man: 'Ok, but for that price I want it with all the options.'

Hillary: 'Great. Oh, and one more thing…The house we wanted last year is back on the market. They're asking $950,000.'

Man: 'Well, then go ahead and make them an offer, but just offer $900,000.'

Hillary: 'Ok. I'll see you later. I love you.'

Man: 'Bye, I love you, too.'

The man hung up. The other men in the locker room were looking at him in astonishment. Then he smiled and asked: 'Anyone know whose phone this is?'

Words of wisdom

Hillary is famous for the waspish comments she makes in private. Some of the caustic remarks attributed to her include the following:

- Men are like placemats: they only show up when there's food on the table.
- 'Easy' is the word used to describe a woman with the sexual morals of a man.
- Email is like a penis. Those who have it would be devastated if it was cut off.

Q: Why do little boys whine?

A: Because they're practising to be men.

Q: How many men does it take to screw in a light bulb?

A: One – he just holds it up there and waits for the world to revolve around him.

or

A: Three – one to screw the bulb, and two to listen to him brag about the screwing part.

forward thinking

Hillary decided to have her portrait painted. She told the artist, 'Paint me with diamond rings, a diamond necklace, emerald bracelets, a ruby brooch and a gold Rolex.'

'But you are not wearing any of those things,' he replied.

'I know,' she said. 'It's just in case I die before Bill. I'm sure he will remarry right away, and I want his new wife to go crazy looking for the jewellery.'

He said, she said

Bill said to Hillary: 'Shall we try a different position tonight?'

Hillary answered: 'That's a good idea: you stand by the ironing board while I sit on the sofa and drink beer.'

Bill said: 'You will never find another man like me.'

Hillary answered: 'Who's gonna look?'

Bill said: 'Why don't you tell me when you have an orgasm?'

Hillary replied: 'I would, but you're never there.'

Breakfast

Hillary was making a breakfast of fried eggs for Bill. Suddenly her husband burst into the kitchen, 'Careful. CAREFUL. Put in some more butter. Oh my GOD. You're cooking too many at once. TOO MANY. Turn them. TURN THEM NOW. We need more butter. Oh my GOD. WHERE are we going to get MORE BUTTER? They're going to STICK. Careful. CAREFUL. I said be CAREFUL. You NEVER listen to me when you're cooking. Never. Turn them. Are you CRAZY? Have you LOST your mind? Don't forget to salt them. You know you always forget to salt them. Use the salt. USE THE SALT. THE SALT.'

Hillary stared at him: 'What the heck is wrong with you? You don't think I know how to fry a couple of eggs?'

Bill calmly replied: 'I just wanted to show you what it feels like when I'm driving.'

Forgiven not forgotten?

Once upon a time in their marriage, Bill did something really stupid. Hillary chewed him out for it and Bill spent a few nights on the couch. Bill apologised and they made up. However, from time to time, Hillary mentioned what he had done. 'Honey,' Bill finally said one day, 'why do you keep bringing that up? I thought your policy was "forgive and forget".'

Hillary replied, 'It is. I just don't want you to forget that I've forgiven and forgotten.'

Agony aunt

Dear Frankie,

My husband is a liar and a cheat. He has cheated on me from the beginning. When I ask him, he denies everything. What's worse is that everyone knows he cheats on me. It is humiliating. Also, since he lost his job a few years ago, he hasn't even looked for a new one. All he does is sit around the living-room in his underwear and watch TV while I work to pay the bills. And, since our daughter went away to college he doesn't even pretend to like me. He keeps calling me a lesbian. What should I do???

Signed, clueless.

Dear clueless,

Dump him. You're a New York Senator now. You don't need him anymore.

Fortune's fool

Hillary Clinton recently went to a fortune-teller who intoned, 'Prepare to become a widow. Your husband will soon suffer a violent death.'

Hillary took a deep breath and asked, 'Will I be acquitted?'

Forward thinking

When Chelsea was eight, Bill and Hillary asked her about her plans for the future. Chelsea said that she would like to attend Harvard. Pleased with her response, they pressed on, 'What would you like to take when you attend college?'

After giving it some thought and glancing around the kitchen, Chelsea replied, 'The refrigerator, if you can get along without it.'

Call me

A young Hillary to Bill: 'Darling, if we get engaged will you give me a ring?'

'Sure,' replied Bill, 'what's your phone number?'

Top five Hillary Clinton campaign slogans

1. Read My Lips – No New Interns.
2. Reward me for putting up with Bill for so long.
3. Isn't it time you were disappointed by a different Clinton?
4. Ask not what your country can do for you, ask how you can illegally contribute to my campaign?
5. Vote for me or my husband will 'greet' your wife.

The stamp of disapproval

The US Postal Service created a stamp with a picture of Senator Hillary Clinton. Once it was in daily use, the stamp would not stick to envelopes. The enraged Senator Clinton demanded a full investigation. After a month of testing, the Commission produced the following findings:

- The stamp was in perfect order.
- There was nothing wrong with the applied adhesive.
- People were spitting on the wrong side.

Wish unwell

Bill and Hillary came upon a wishing-well. Hillary leaned over, made a wish and threw in a penny. Her husband decided to make a wish, too. But he leaned over too far, fell into the well and drowned.

Hillary was stunned for a moment but then smiled, 'It really works'.

Chapter 17 By George

George Bush speaks more from the heart than the brain. Through his dubious deeds and his many mishaps, misdemeanours and miscalculations, he has enriched the lives of the political and chattering classes. There have been many occasions when he would have benefited from taking Mark Twain's advice: 'Better to keep your mouth shut and appear stupid than to open it and remove all doubt.' Bush has carved out a unique place for himself on the political landscape. The following stories capture some of the essence of Dubya.

That feeling of achievement

Dick Cheney walked into the Oval Office and saw the President whooping and hollering.

'What's the matter, Mr President?' inquired the Vice President.

'Nothing at all, boss. I just done finished a jigsaw puzzle in record time!' the President beamed.

'How long did it take you?'

'Well, the box said "3 to 5 years" but I did it in a month!'

These boots were made for walking

When George Bush was a little boy, he asked his kindergarten teacher for help putting on his cowboy boots. Even with her pulling and him pushing, the little boots still didn't want to go on. Finally, after working up a sweat, she got the second boot on. She almost cried when the little boy said, 'Teacher, they're on the wrong feet'. She looked and, sure enough, they were. It wasn't any easier pulling the boots off than it was putting them on. She managed to keep her cool, and together they worked to get the boots back on, this time on the right feet.

Little George then announced, 'These aren't my boots.'

The teacher bit her tongue. Once again, she struggled to help him pull the ill-fitting boots off his little feet. No sooner had they got the boots off than he said, 'They're my brother's boots. My mom made me wear them.'

She didn't know whether to laugh or cry. However, she mustered up the grace and courage she had left to wrestle the boots on his feet again.

Helping him into his coat, she asked, 'Now, where are your mittens?'

He said, 'I stuffed them in the toes of my boots.'

An American in Paris

A special G8 Summit was being held in Paris over a two-week period. The world leaders decided to set an example by foregoing their normal lavish banquets. Instead they had their wives make them sandwiches. By the end of the fortnight, the leaders could take no more.

Jacques Chirac, Tony Blair and George Bush were having their lunch on the top of the Eiffel Tower. Before he opened his lunchbox, Chirac told the other two: 'If my wife has made me those damn lamb sandwiches for 14 days in a row, I will kill myself.' Alas, when he opened his lunchbox it was lamb again, so he jumped off the tower.

Next up was Tony Blair, who said: 'If Cherie has made me those blasted beef sandwiches for 14 days in a row, I will kill myself.' Sadly, when he opened his lunchbox it was indeed beef, so he jumped off the tower. Then it was Bush's turn: 'If I have those horrible French snails for lunch for 14 days in a row, I will kill myself.' Tragically, the sandwiches were indeed French snails and Dubya shuffled off this mortal coil by jumping off the tower.

When an official on the tower relayed a verbatim account of what had happened to the American delegation, everyone in the room turned reproachfully to the new widow. Mrs Bush calmly stated: 'I don't know what you are looking at me for. George always made his own sandwiches.'

Lost in translation

Today President Bush had a meeting with Russian President Vladimir Putin. The meeting had two translators, and they still had a rough time. The difficulty was finding the Russian for 'okie dokie'.

It's only words

George Bush found himself talking to a linguistics professor. The academic said, 'In English a double negative forms a positive. However, in some languages, such as Russian, a double negative is still a negative. However, there is no language wherein a double positive can form a negative.'

With a baffled look on his face, Bush piped up, 'Yeah, right'.

Lost

George Bush and his wife were driving in Canada and got lost. Finally they came into a city. They saw an old man on the street, and Laura let down her car window and asked, 'Excuse me, Sir. Can you tell me where we are?' The man replied, 'Saskatoon, Saskatchewan.'

As Laura rolled up the window, George turned to her and said, 'We really are lost. They don't even speak English here.'

It doesn't add up

At New York's International Airport yesterday an individual, later discovered to be a teacher, was arrested trying to board a flight while in possession of a ruler, protractor, setsquare, slide rule and calculator. At a morning press conference, Attorney John Ashcroft said he believed the man to be a member of the notorious Al-Gebra movement. The FBI is charging him with carrying weapons of maths instruction.

'Al-Gebra is a fearsome cult,' Ashcroft said. 'They desire average solutions by means and extremes, and sometimes go off on tangents in search of absolute values. They use code names like 'X' and 'Y' and refer to themselves as 'unknowns', but we have determined that they belong to a common denominator of the axis of medieval with coordinates in every country. As the Greek philanderer Isosceles used to say, 'There are three sides to every triangle.'

When asked to comment on the arrest, President Bush said, 'If God had wanted us to have better weapons of maths instruction, he would have given us more fingers and toes.'

Novel cuisine
Condoleeza Rice made her last stop on her foreign trip in Beijing. They went nuts for her. From their reaction, you would think people in China had never seen Rice before.

Mixed blessing
President Dubya was awakened one night by an urgent call from the Pentagon. 'Mr President,' said the four-star general, barely able to contain himself, 'there's good news and bad news.'

'Oh, no,' muttered the President. 'Well, let me have the bad news first.'

'The bad news, Sir, is that we've been invaded by creatures from another planet.'

'Gosh, and the good news?'

'The good news, Sir, is that they eat reporters and pee oil.'

Why, oh why?
Q: Why is George Bush proof of reincarnation?
A: You just can't get that screwed up in one lifetime.
Q: Why does George Bush open yoghurt cartons while still in the supermarket?
A: Because the lid says 'Open Here'.
Q: Why was George Bush unusual from birth?
A: His mother had morning sickness after he was born.
Q: Why does Dubya spend so much time staring at glasses of orange juice?
A: Because it says, 'concentrate' on the carton.

Furniture removal
Relatives sympathised when Mrs Bush complained that her back was really sore from moving furniture.

'Why didn't you wait till your husband got home to move it?' someone asked.

'I could have, but the couch is easier to move if he's not on it.'

Active age

George Bush Sr had worked hard for so long, so Dubya was more than a little curious about how his dad filled his days since his retirement. 'How has life changed?' he asked.

Bush Sr replied, 'Well, I get up in the morning with nothing to do, and I got to bed at night with it half done.'

Excitement

In 2005, Laura Bush addressed political journalists. She told them that her husband, whom she termed 'Mr Excitement', goes to bed at 9 pm while she stays up and watches *Desperate Housewives*. As a result, she said, she felt like a desperate housewife herself.

The First Lady intimated that, if George wanted to win the war on terror, he would have to stay up later. She also tried to shatter the myth, cherished by some Republicans, that George is a brilliant rancher. According to his wife, Dubya's solution to any problem on the ranch is to mow it down. That is why his daughters call him 'The Texas Chainsaw Massacre'.

In the arms of an angel

George Bush: 'My wife's an angel.'
Bill Clinton: 'You're lucky. Mine's still alive.'

Family values

George Bush and Bill Clinton were discussing their attitudes to sex, marriage and family values. Bush said, 'I didn't sleep with my wife until we got married. Did you?'

Clinton responded, 'I'm not sure. What was her maiden name?'

True confessions

Bill Clinton: 'My wife got me to believe in religion.'
George Bush: 'Really?'

Bill Clinton: 'Yeah. Until I married her I didn't believe in hell.'

Hair today

George W. Bush and Bill Clinton somehow ended up at the same barbershop. As they sat there, each being worked on by a different barber, not a word was spoken. The barbers were both afraid to start a conversation, for fear it would turn to politics. As the barbers finished their shaves, the one who had Clinton in his chair reached for the aftershave.

Clinton was quick to stop him saying, 'No thanks, my wife will smell that and think I've been in a whorehouse.'

The second barber turned to Bush and said, 'How about you?'

Bush replied, 'Go ahead, my wife doesn't know what the inside of a whorehouse smells like.'

The windy city

George Bush travelled to London to meet Queen Elizabeth. The Queen took him on a tour of the city in a horse-drawn carriage. One of the horses let out a thunderous, cataclysmic fart that reverberated through the air and rattled the doors of the coach. Uncomfortable, the two powerful figures focused their attention elsewhere and behaved as if nothing had happened. But the Queen was the first to realise that ignoring what had just happened was ridiculous.

She explained, 'Mr President, please accept my regrets. I'm sure you understand that there are some things that even a Queen cannot control.'

President Bush replied, 'Your Majesty, please don't give the matter another thought. You know, if you hadn't said something I would have thought it was one of the horses.'

A biblical epic

George W. was in an airport lobby and noticed a man in a long, flowing white robe with a flowing white beard and flowing white hair. The man had a staff in one hand and ten tablets under the other arm.

Dubya approached the man and inquired, 'Aren't you Moses?'

The man ignored Dubya and stared at the ceiling.

George positioned himself more directly in the man's view and asked again, 'Are you Moses?'

The man continued to peruse the ceiling.

George tugged at the man's sleeve and asked again, 'Aren't you Moses?'

The man finally responded in an irritated voice, 'Yes, I am'.

Dubya asked him why he was so uppity and the man replied, 'The last time a bush spoke to me I ended up spending 40 years in the wilderness.'

Heavenly fury

God was fed up. In a crash of thunder he yanked up three influential men to heaven: George Bush, Vladimir Putin and Bill Gates.

'The human race is a complete disappointment,' God boomed. 'You each have one week to prepare your followers for the End of the World.' With another crash of thunder, the men found themselves back on Earth.

Bush immediately called his cabinet. 'I have good news and bad news,' he announced grimly. 'The good news is that there is a God. The bad news is that he's really mad and plans to end the world in a week.'

In Russia, Putin announced to parliament, 'I have bad news and worse news. The bad news is that we were wrong – there is a God after all. The worse news is that he's mad and is going to end the world in a week.'

Meanwhile, Bill Gates called a meeting of his top engineers. 'I have good news and better news. The good news is that God considers me one of the three most influential men on Earth,' he beamed. 'The better news is that we don't have to fix Windows 2005.

War on terror

Before war was declared in Iraq, President Bush and Secretary Powell were sitting in a bar. A guy walked in and asked the barman, 'Isn't that Bush and Powell sitting over there?'

The barman said, 'Yep, that's them.'

So the guy walked over and said, 'Wow, this is a real honour. What are you guys doing?'

Bush said, 'We're planning WWIII'.

And the man said, 'Really? What's going to happen?'

Bush says, 'Well, we're going to kill 140 million Iraqis this time and one blonde with really big boobs.'

The man exclaimed, 'A blonde with big boobs? Why kill a blonde with those credentials?'

Bush turned to Powell, punched him on the shoulder and said, 'See? I told you no one would worry about the 140 million Iraqis'.

The tourist

A Bedouin wandering in the Sahara happened upon George Bush dressed in a bathing suit, flip-flops, a big, over-sized t-shirt and sunglasses.

The Bedouin gazed at him in amazement, 'What are you doing all the way out here dressed like that?'

'I'm going swimming,' Bush explained.

'But the ocean is 800 miles away,' the Arab informed him.

'Eight hundred miles!' Bush exclaimed with a whistle of appreciation. 'Boy, what a beach!'

Bright spark

Given Bush's intellectual limitations, some people have wondered how he progressed through the American academic system. Using the Freedom of Information of Act, I have managed to obtain a copy of his entrance exam, which is reproduced below:

College Entrance Exam for Members of the Bush family

You must Answer **Two** (2) or More Questions Correctly to Qualify

1.   What language is spoken in France?
2.   (a) Give a dissertation on the ancient Babylonian Empire with particular reference to architecture, literature, law and social conditions.

OR

(b) Write the first name of PIERRE Trudeau.

3. Would you ask William Shakespeare to: (a) build a bridge (b) sail an ocean (c) lead an army (d) WRITE A PLAY?

4. What religion is the Pope? (Circle only one) (a) Jewish (b) CATHOLIC (c) Hindu (d) Swedish (e) Agnostic.

5. Metric conversion. How many feet in 0.0 metres?

6. What time is it when the big hand is on the 12 and the small hand is on the 1?

7. How many commandments was Moses given? (Approximate)

8. What are people called in the far north of the United States? (a) Westerners (b) Southerners (C) NORTHENERS.

9. Spell the following words: CAT, DOG, PIG.

10. Six kings of England have been called George, the last one being George the Sixth. Name the previous five.

EXTRA CREDIT: Using your fingers, count from 1 to 5.

Testing times

When Bush was in college, he took an important exam. His friend Bubba was in the same class, having entered the prestigious academic institution on the basis of a sports scholarship. Bubba was worried. He was on academic probation and would not be allowed to play in the big football game the following week unless he passed the exam.

The test was a 'fill in the blanks'; the last question read: 'Old MacDonald had a _____.' Bubba was stumped. He had no idea what to answer, and he knew he had to get this one right to be sure he passed. Making sure the professor wasn't watching, he tapped Bush on the shoulder and whispered, 'George, what's the answer to the last question?' Bush laughed, then looked around to check that the professor hadn't noticed. He turned to Bubba and in a low voice said, 'Bubba, you're so stupid. Everyone knows that Old MacDonald had a farm.'

'Oh yeah,' said Bubba, 'I remember now.' He picked up his pen and started to write the answer in the blank. Then he stopped. Tapping Bush on the shoulder, he whispered, 'George, how do you spell farm?'

'You really are dumb, Bubba. That's so easy,' hissed Dubya. 'Farm is E-I-E-I-O.'

When in Madrid

One day, Bush assembled his 'coalition of the willing' in Madrid to rally support for the Gulf War. After his day of lobbying, Dubya stopped at a local restaurant. While sipping his beer, he noticed a sizzling, scrumptious-looking platter being served at the next table. Not only did the food look good, it smelled wonderful. George asked the waiter, 'What is that you just served?' The waiter replied, 'Ah, Señor, you have excellent taste. Those are bull's balls from the bullfight this morning. A delicacy.'

Though momentarily daunted when he learned the origin of the dish, Dubya said, 'What the hell, I'm sort of on a vacation. Bring me an order.'

The waiter replied, 'I am so sorry, Señor. There is only one serving a day, since there is only one bullfight each morning. If you come early tomorrow and place your order, we will be sure to serve you this delicacy.'

The next morning, Bush returned, placed his order and was served the one and only special delicacy of the day. After a few bites, and having inspected the contents of his platter, he called to the waiter and said, 'These are much, much smaller than the ones I saw you serve yesterday!'

The waiter promptly replied, 'Sí, Señor. Sometimes the bull wins!'

Fathers and daughters

Dubya's daughters have made the headlines for their fondness for drink. It is said that the security arrangements for the last presidential inauguration were the most extensive in history. And that was just to keep the Bush twins away from the bar.

Big news

After Laura had just given birth, George Bush ran out of the delivery room and announced to the rest of his family, 'We had twins!'

The family were so excited they immediately asked, 'Who do they look like?'

George looked puzzled and then said, 'Each other'.

The late, late show

Late one Saturday night, George Bush was awakened by the phone ringing. In a sleepy, grumpy voice he said hello. The party on the other end of the line paused for a moment, before rushing breathlessly into a lengthy speech.

'Dad, this is Trisha and I'm sorry I woke you up, but I had to call because I'm going to be a little late getting home. See, Mom's car has a fault but it's not my fault. Honest, I don't know what happened. The tyre just went flat while we were inside the disco. Please don't be mad, okay?'

'I'm sorry, dear,' Bush replied, 'but you've reached the wrong number. I don't have a daughter named Trisha.'

'Wow, Dad,' the young woman replied, 'I didn't think you'd be this mad.'

Strong drink

Bush decided to go on a 'meet the people tour'. He went into a 24-hour mini-mart to get himself a cup of freshly brewed coffee. When he picked up the pot, the President could not help noticing that the brew was as black as asphalt and just about as thick.

'How old is the coffee you have here?' he asked the woman who was standing behind the store counter.

She shrugged, 'I don't know. I've only been working here for two weeks.'

The top 12 Bushisms

After the war against terror, some people have suggested that George W. Bush should be put on trial for war crimes. It is more likely that in some future date he will be put on trial for crimes against the English language. The following are perhaps the 12 best Bushisms.

1. They misunderestimated me.

2. They want the federal government controlling social security like it's some kind of federal program.

3. This is an impressive crowd. The haves and the have-mores. Some people call you the elite. I call you my base.

4. That's a chapter [the Lewinsky scandal], the last chapter of the twentieth, twentieth, the twenty-first century that most of us would rather forget. The last chapter of the twentieth century. This is the first chapter of the twenty-first century.

5. The vast majority of our imports come from outside the country.

6. If we don't succeed, we run the risk of failure.

7. The French don't have a word for 'entrepreneur'.

8. I have made good judgements in the past. I have made good judgements in the future.

9. We're going to have the best-educated American people in the world.

10. A low voter turnout is an indication of fewer people going to the polls.

11. It isn't pollution that is harming the environment. It's the impurities in our air and water that are doing it.

12. I stand by the misstatements that I've made.

Chapter 18 Born in the USA

It is a truth universally acknowledged that Americans do things on a bigger scale than everybody else. They can be very egocentric, as in the observation of Sam Walton, founder of Wal-mart: 'I was asked what I thought about the recession. I thought about it and decided not to take part.' They do things in America that visitors find puzzling:

In America, why:

- Can a pizza get to your house faster than an ambulance?
- Are there disabled parking places in front of a skating rink?
- Do drugstores make the sick walk all the way to the back of the shop to get their prescriptions, while healthy people can buy cigarettes at the front?
- Do people order double cheeseburgers, large fries and a Diet Coke?
- Do banks leave both doors open and then chain the pens to the counters?
- Do they leave cars worth thousands of dollars in the driveway and put their useless junk in the garage?
- Do they use answering machines to screen calls and then have call waiting so they won't miss a call from someone they didn't want to talk to in the first place?

Americans can also be unintentionally hilarious, as the following exchange demonstrates:

Lawyer: 'Do you suffer from memory lapses?'
Michael Jackson: 'Not that I recall.'

American politics is largely about establishing the United States' superiority, while putting down its opponents. The following pages capture a flavour of this unique political culture.

The Dan Quayle school of history

During his term as Vice President, Dan Quayle became famous for his willingness to impart knowledge whenever he visited schools. Here are some of the unusual understandings of history attributed to him.

1. Queen Elizabeth was the 'Virgin Queen'. As a queen she was a great success. When she exposed herself before her troops they all shouted 'hurrah'.

2. The Middle Ages were an era of great inventions and discoveries. Gutenberg invented removable type and the Bible. Another important invention was the circulation of blood. Sir Walter Raleigh is a historical figure because he invented cigarettes and started smoking.

3. The greatest writer of the Renaissance was William Shakespeare. He was born in the year 1564, supposedly on his birthday. He never made much money and is famous only because of his plays. He wrote tragedies, comedies and hysterectomies, all in Islamic pentameter. Romeo and Juliet are an example of a heroic couplet.

4. Writing at the same time as Shakespeare was Miguel de Cervantes. He wrote *Donkey Hote*. The next great author was John Milton. Milton wrote *Paradise Lost*. Then his wife died and he wrote *Paradise Regained*.

5. One of the causes of the Revolutionary War was that the English put tacks in their tea. Also, the colonists could send their parcels through the post without stamps. Finally, the colonists won the war and no longer had to pay for taxis. Thomas Jefferson and Benjamin Franklin were two singers of the Declaration of Independence. Franklin discovered electricity by rubbing two cats backwards and declared, 'A horse divided against itself cannot stand'. Franklin died in 1790 and is still dead.

6. Johann Bach wrote a great many musical compositions and had a large number of children. In between, he practised on an old spinster which he kept up in his attic. Bach died from 1750 to the present. Bach was the most famous composer in the world and so was Handel. Handel was half German and half Italian and half English. He was very large.

7. Beethoven wrote music even though he was deaf. He was so deaf he wrote loud music. He took long walks in the forest even when everybody was calling for him. He expired in 1827 and later died from this.

8. The nineteenth century was a time of great many thoughts and inventions. People stopped reproducing by hand and started reproducing by machine. The invention of the steamboat caused a network of rivers to spring up. Cyrus McCormick invented the McCormick raper, which did the work of a hundred men.

9. Louis Pasteur discovered a cure for rabbis. Charles Darwin was a naturalist who wrote *The Organ of the Species*. Madam Curie discovered radio. And Karl Marx became one of the Marx Brothers.

10. The First World War, caused by the assignation of the Arch-Duck by an anarchist, ushered in a new error in the anals of human history.

Exclusive

Hot off the presses. We can exclusively reveal that former American Vice President, Dan Quayle, is about to enter the race to succeed George W. Bush as President. His manifesto is unique. The Top 10 Dan Quayle Campaign Promises are as follows (When it was pointed out to Dan that these were a dozen promises and not 10, he asked, 'are there not 10 in a dozen?'):

12. Support NATOE.
11. Reduce the number of commercials on the Cartoon Network.
10. Statehood for Hawaii and Alaska.
9. Four years of unequalled prosperity for comedy writers.

8. To lead this great nation into the 20th century.

7. New safety campaign: Scissors Is Pointy.

6. A peaceful end to the Vietnam war.

5. Appoint Judge Reinhold (the actor and star of the *Beverly Hills Cop* series) to the Supreme Court.

4. Spending cuts – except for funding of this cool rocket car idea I came up with.

3. More bondage between parents and children.

2. By the end of my term, America will be fully prepared for the Y2K bug.

1. Read my lips: Know new taxis!

The first lady

America had just appointed its first Jewish female President. The first crisis arose for the incumbent when her mother threatened not to come to the inauguration ceremony. She claimed that it is too awkward for her to travel all the way from her home in California.

'Don't worry about it, Mom, I'll send Air Force One to fly you up and take you home. And a limousine will pick you up at your door.'

'I don't know. Everybody will be so fancy, I don't know what on earth I would wear.'

'Oh, Mom, don't worry about it. I'll make sure you have a wonderful gown by Christian Dior.'

'Honey, you know I can't stand those rich foods you and your friends like to eat.'

'Don't worry, Mom. The entire affair is going to be handled by the best caterer in New York, kosher all the way. Mom, I want you to come.'

So Mom agreed and, on 19 January 2013, Sarah Levinson was sworn in as President of the USA. In the front row sat the new President's mother, who leaned over to a senator sitting next to her, 'You see that woman over there with her hand on the Bible, becoming President of the United States?'

The senator whispered back, 'Yes I do.'

'Her brother's a doctor.'

The beautiful game

A coach had put together the perfect American football team, missing only a top-class quarterback. He had scouted all the colleges and the Canadian and European leagues, but he couldn't find the player to guarantee a Super Bowl win. One night he was watching a war-zone scene in Iraq on TV. In the background of one shot, he saw a young Iraqi soldier with a truly incredible arm. He threw a hand grenade straight into a 15th story window 100 yards away. KABOOM.

He threw another grenade 75 yards, pitching it right into a chimney. KA-BLOOEY.

Then he threw another into a car passing at 90 miles per hour. Bull's eye.

'I've got to get this guy!' the coach shouted. 'He's got the perfect arm.'

The coach found the soldier, brought him to the States and taught him the great game of football. The team went on to win the Super Bowl. The young Iraqi was hailed as a great hero, and when the coach asked him what he wanted, he said he wanted to call his mother.

'Mom,' he said into the phone, 'I just won the Super Bowl.'

'I don't want to talk to you,' the old Muslim woman snapped. 'You are not my son.'

'You don't understand, Mother. I've won the greatest sporting event in the world. I'm here among thousands of my adoring fans.'

'No. Let me tell you. At this very moment, there are gunshots all around us. The neighbourhood is a pile of rubble. The elections are a joke, your two brothers were beaten within an inch of their lives last week, and I have to keep your sister in the house so she doesn't get raped.'

The old lady paused, then tearfully added, 'I will never forgive you for making us move to Philadelphia'.

The moral maze

Here is a moral dilemma. The situation: An American is in the Middle East, and there is a huge flood. Many thousands of people have died, water supplies have been compromised and buildings destroyed.

The American is a freelance photographer and is taking photos for a news service. He is travelling around looking for particularly poignant scenes, when he comes across Osama Bin Laden who has been swept up by the floodwaters. Bin Laden is barely hanging on to a tree limb and is about to go under. The photographer can either put down his camera and save him, or take a Pulitzer Prize–winning photo of him as he loses his grip on the branch.

This is his moral quandary: which lens and shutter speed should he use?

With a little help from our friends

The Canadians pledged to help America with the war on terror. They pledged two battleships, 600 ground troops and six fighter jets.

With the American exchange rate, the Yanks ended up with two canoes, six Mounties and a bunch of flying squirrels.

Revelations

Under the Freedom of Information Act, I have been able to establish the real reason why NATO went to war in Kosovo in the 1990s. On that fateful day, the US Defence Secretary Madeline Albright, a formidable intellect but not a beauty queen, walked into the NATO meeting, saw that she was the only female in the room and asked: 'So gentlemen, shall we make love or war?'

The vote was unanimous.

Puppy love

After Al Gore controversially lost the 2000 presidential race to George Bush a new joke surfaced:

Q: What's the difference between Al Gore and a puppy?

A: After five weeks, the puppy will open its eyes and stop whining.

Flying without wings

In the 2004presidential campaign, John Kerry visited a Native American reservation. He was greeted by an old Indian chief who, with great ceremony, gave him the name 'Running Eagle'. Kerry was thrilled. His good humour did not last after tribal officials explained that a Running Eagle is a bird so full of crap it can't fly.

During the course of that campaign, Kerry received another unusual endorsement when he attended Mass at Washington Cathedral. During his homily the cardinal observed, 'John Kerry is petty, a self-absorbed hypocrite and a nitwit. He is a liar, a cheat and a windbag. He is the worst example of a Catholic I've personally every known. But compared to Ted Kennedy, John Kerry is a saint.'

Low maintenance

When John Kerry divorced his first wife, the judge said, 'Mr Kerry, I have reviewed this case very carefully. And I've decided to give your wife $775 a week.'

Kerry answered, 'That's very fair, your honour. And every now and then I'll try to send her a few bucks myself.'

Position vacant

The CIA had an opening for an assassin. After all the background checks, interviews and testing were done, there were three finalists – two men and one woman. For the final test, the CIA agents took one of the men to a large metal door and handed him a gun.

'We must know that you will follow instructions, no matter what the circumstances. Inside this room you will find your wife sitting in a chair. You have to kill her.' The first man said, 'You can't be serious. I could never shoot my wife.'

The agent replied, 'Then you are not the right man for the job.'

The second man was given the same instructions. He took the gun and went into the room. All was quiet for about five minutes. Then the agent came out with tears in his eyes. 'I tried, but I can't kill my wife,' he said. The agent told him, 'You don't have what it takes. Get your wife and go home.'

Finally, it was the woman's turn. She was told to kill her husband. She took the gun into the room. Shots were heard, one shot after another. The agents heard screaming, crashing, banging on the walls.

After a few minutes all was quiet. The door opened slowly and there stood the woman with sweat dripping from her brow and she said, 'You didn't tell me the gun was loaded with blanks, so I beat him to death with the chair'.

It's the end

It may depress you to imagine what will happen when the end of the world arrives. Not the American media – most already have their headlines ready:

USA Today: We're Dead

The Wall Street Journal: Dow Jones Plummets as World Ends

National Enquirer: OJ and Nicole, Together Again

Microsoft Systems Journal: Apple Loses Market Share

Victoria's Secret Catalogue: Our Final Sale

Sports Illustrated: Game Over

Wired: The Last New Thing

Rolling Stone: The Grateful Dead Reunion Tour

Readers Digest: BYE

Discover Magazine: How will the extinction of all life as we know it affect the way we view the cosmos?

Lady's Home Journal: Lose 10 lbs by judgement day with our new 'Armageddon' diet

America Online: System temporarily down. Try calling back in 15 minutes.

Inc. magazine: Ten ways you can profit from the apocalypse

TIME magazine: Renew your subscription for eternity

Mixed messages

During a particularly icy winter, a Minneapolis couple decided to go to Florida to thaw out. They planned to stay at the same hotel where they had spent their honeymoon 20 years earlier. Because of hectic schedules, it was difficult to coordinate their travel arrangements. So, the husband left Minnesota and flew to Florida on Thursday, with his wife flying down the following day.

The husband checked into the hotel. There was a computer in his room, so he decided to send an email to his wife. However, he accidentally left out one letter in her email address, and without realising his error, sent the email.

Meanwhile, somewhere in Houston, Texas, a widow had just returned home from her husband's funeral. He was a senator who died following a heart attack. The widow decided to check her email, expecting messages from relatives and friends. After reading the first message, she screamed and fainted. Her son rushed into her room, found his mother on the floor, and saw the computer screen which read:

To: My Loving Wife
Subject: I've arrived
Date: October 14, 2005

I know you're surprised to hear from me. They have computers here now and you are allowed to send emails. I've just arrived and have checked in. I see that everything has been prepared for your arrival tomorrow. Looking forward to seeing you then.
Hope your journey is as uneventful as mine was.

P.S. Sure is freaking hot down here!

Time to say goodbye

A former US senator loved the perks of the job. However, after two terms in the Senate he was forced to retire because of sickness and tiredness. The voters were sick and tired of him. Given the sudden drop in his family finances he strongly 'encouraged' his wife to return to the workforce. He decided to devote his attention to writing his memoirs. Political scientists were offered them but, as they were sanctimonious, self-serving and mind-numbingly boring, they quickly discarded them. The one chapter that people read with some interest was his reflection on married life. An abridged version now follows:

Shortly after she returned to work, I noticed my wife was beginning to show her age. I usually get home from the golf course about the same time she gets home from work. Although she knows how hungry I am, she almost always says she has to rest for half an hour before she starts dinner. I don't yell at her. Instead, I tell her to take her time and just wake me when she gets dinner on the table. I generally have lunch in the men's grill at the club, so I'm ready for some home-cooked grub when I hit that door...

She used to do the dishes as soon as we finished eating. But now it's not unusual for them to sit on the table for several hours after dinner. I do what I can by diplomatically reminding her several times each evening that they won't clean themselves. I know she appreciates this, as it does seem to motivate her to get them done before she goes to bed. I really think my old business as a leading politician helps a lot. I consider telling people what they ought to do one of my strong points.

I know that I probably sound like a saint in the way I support Sue. I'm not saying that showing this much consideration is easy. Many men will find it difficult. Some will find it impossible! Nobody knows better than I do, how frustrating women become as they get older.

However, guys, even if you show just a little more tact and less criticism of your ageing wife because of this book, I will consider that writing it was well worthwhile. After all, we are put on this earth to help each other...

Author's note: the former senator died suddenly on Thursday, November 3. He was found with a 50-inch Big Bertha Driver rammed up his rectum with only two inches of the grip showing. His wife Sue was arrested, but the grand jury accepted her defence that he accidentally sat on it. She was released on Friday, November 4.

Economy of language

President Calvin Coolidge, 30th US President (1923–29), was a man of very few words. One Sunday, he went to church, but his wife,

Grace, stayed home. When he returned home, she asked, 'Was the sermon good?'

'Yup,' was Coolidge's brief reply.

'What was it about?' Grace asked.

'Sin.'

'And what did the minister say?'

'He's against it.'

Republicans and Democrats: How to tell the difference

Democrats mostly buy books that have been banned somewhere.
Republicans form censorship committees and read books as a group.

Democrats give their worn out clothes to the less fortunate.
Republicans wear theirs.

Democrats name their children after currently popular sports figures, politicians and entertainers.
Republican children are named after their parents or grandparents, depending on whose side of the family the money is.

Republicans tend to keep their shades drawn, although there is seldom any reason why they should.
Democrats ought to, but don't.

Republican boys date Democratic girls. They plan to marry Republican girls, but feel that they're entitled to a little fun first.

Democrats make plans and then do something else.
Republicans follow the plans their grandfathers made.

Republican couples sleep in twin beds – some even in separate rooms.
That is why there are more Democrats.

Three lovely ladies

A Republican senator and a born-again Christian had three virgin daughters. They were all getting married, and Dad was a bit worried about how their sex life would get started. He made them all promise to send a postcard from the honeymoon with a few words on how the marital lovemaking was going.

Two days after the wedding the first daughter sent a card from her honeymoon in Hawaii. The card said nothing but 'Nescafé'. At first Dad was puzzled, but he got his wife to go into the kitchen and get out the Nescafé jar. It said: 'Good 'til the last drop'. Dad blushed, but was pleased for his daughter.

The second daughter sent her card from Vienna a week after the wedding. The card said simply: 'Marlboro'. The senator pulled out his cigarette box from his pocket, and he read from the pack: 'Extra Long. King Size.' Again the senator was a bit embarrassed, but pleased for his girl.

The third daughter left for her honeymoon in Jamaica. The senator waited for a week, and nothing. Another week went by and still nothing. The senator started to get really worried. Then after a month, the card finally arrived. Written on it with shaky handwriting were the words 'British Airways'.

The senator took out his wife's latest *Harpers Bazaar* magazine, and flipped through the pages fearing the worst. Finally he found the ad for BA. The ad said: 'Three times a day, seven days a week, both ways.'

The senator fainted.

Different reactions

The NYPD, the FBI and the CIA were all trying to prove that they are best at apprehending criminals. The President decided to give them a test. He released a rabbit into a forest and told each organisation to catch it.

The CIA went in. They placed animal informants throughout the forest. They questioned all plant and mineral witnesses. After three months of extensive investigations, they concluded that rabbits do not exist.

The FBI went in. After two weeks with no leads they burned the forest, killing everything in it, including the rabbit, and they made no apologies. The rabbit had it coming.

The NYPD went in. They came out two hours later with a badly beaten bear. The bear was yelling: 'Okay. I'm a rabbit. I'm a rabbit!'

Protected species

In America political correctness reigns supreme. This sometimes presents employers with problems. An American boss told four of his employees: 'I'm really sorry, but I'm going to have to let one of you go.'

African-American employee: 'I'm a protected minority.'

Female employee: 'And I'm a woman.'

Oldest employee: 'Fire me, buster, and I'll hit you with an age discrimination suit so fast it'll make your head spin.'

To which they all turned to look at the helpless young, white male employee, who thought for a moment, then responded: 'I think I might be gay...'

Diversion

This is the transcript of the actual radio conversation between a US naval ship and Canadian authorities off the coast of Newfoundland in October 1995.

Canadians: 'Please divert your course 15 degrees to the south to avoid a collision.'

Americans: 'Recommend you divert your course 15 degrees to the north to avoid a collision.'

Canadians: 'Negative. You will have to divert your course 15 degrees to the south to avoid a collision.'

Americans: 'This is the captain of a US naval ship. I say again, divert YOUR course.'

Canadians: 'No. I say again, you divert YOUR course.'

Americans: THIS IS THE AIRCRAFT CARRIER *US LINCOLN*, THE SECOND LARGEST SHIP IN THE UNITES STATES' ATLANTIC FLEET. WE ARE ACCOMPANIED BY THREE DESTROYERS, THREE CRUISERS AND NUMEROUS

SUPPORT VESSELS. I DEMAND THAT YOU CHANGE YOUR COURSE 15 DEGREES NORTH. I SAY AGAIN, THAT'S ONE FIVE DEGREES NORTH, OR COUNTER-MEASURES WILL BE TAKEN TO ENSURE THE SAFETY OF THIS SHIP.'
Canadians: 'This is a lighthouse. Your call!'

Rest in peace

A Congressman died in his sleep and the wife decided to leave him in bed for a week before sending for the doctor. After seven days she rang the medic. 'Doctor, Teddy's been dead for a week.'

'Why didn't you call me before this?' inquired the doctor.

'Well,' said the widow, 'we always promised each other we'd have one quiet week together.'

So long, Marianne

A man was on his deathbed. In a hoarse whisper he said to his wife, 'Marianne, remember how we started that little grocery store in Kiev and the Cossacks drove us out and you were by my side?'

'Yes,' Marianne said.

'And remember how we had the little vegetable stand in Berlin and the Nazis drove us out, and you were by my side?'

'Yes,' Marianne said.

'And remember how we had the meat market in the Bronx and the mafia took over the neighbourhood and our store was fire-bombed and you were by my side?'

'Yes.'

'And remember how we came to Miami and I became governor and I had my heart attack, and you were by my side?'

'Oh yes.'

'Marianne, there's one thing I've always wanted to ask you, and now that I'm dying, I can finally ask it.'

'What is it, my darling?'

'Marianne, are you a jinx?'

Headlines from 2040

- Baby conceived naturally – Scientists stumped.
- Castro finally dies at the age of 112; Cuban cigars can now be imported legally, but President Chelsea Clinton has banned all smoking.
- 35-year, $75.8 billion study: diet and exercise are the keys to weight loss.
- Average height of NBA players now nine feet, seven inches.
- Microsoft announces it has perfected its newest version of Windows, so it crashes BEFORE installation is completed.
- Congress authorises direct deposit of illegal political contributions to campaign accounts.
- Massachusetts executes last remaining conservative.
- Supreme Court rules punishment of criminals violates their civil rights.
- Florida voters still don't know how to use a voting machine.
- 'Born in the USA' becomes the official anthem of the American Territory of the Middle East (formerly known as Iraq, Afghanistan, Syria and Lebanon).
- France pleads for global help after being over taken by Jamaica.
- George Z. Bush announces he will run for President.

Get Carter

This week the US navy named a nuclear submarine after Jimmy Carter. Experts say the sub will be ineffective for four years but tremendously respected once it's retired.

Angel eyes

A senator and his teenage daughter were driving to town in his new car. 'Be an angel, Dad,' said his daughter, 'and let me drive.'

He did. And he is.

Political bumper stickers

- If ignorance is bliss, why aren't more politicians happy?

- Everything should be made as simple as possible, but no simpler.
- Once over the hill, you pick up speed.
- Whatever hits the fan will not be evenly distributed.
- A clear conscience is usually the sign of a bad memory.
- If at first you don't succeed, destroy all evidence that you tried.
- Republicans have a photographic memory. They just don't have a film.

Wisdom from the American military

Aim towards the enemy.

Instruction printed on a US rocket launcher.

When the pin is pulled, Mr Grenade is not our friend.

US Marine Corps leaflet

Cluster bombing from B-52s is very, very accurate. The bombs are guaranteed to always hit the ground.

USAF Ammo Troop

If the enemy is in range, so are you.

The Infantry Journal

A slipping gear could let your M203 grenade launcher fire when you least expect it. That would make you quite unpopular in what's left of your unit.

The US Army's Magazine of Preventive Maintenance

It is generally inadvisable to eject directly over the area you just bombed.

US Air Force Manual

Try to look unimportant; they may be low on ammo.

The Infantry Journal

Tracers work both ways.

US Army Ordnance

Five-second fuses only last three seconds.

The Infantry Journal

If you're attacking is going too well, you're walking into an ambush.

The Infantry Journal

No combat-ready unit has ever passed inspection.

Joe Gay Magazine

Any ship can be a minesweeper – once.

Anonymous

Never tell the platoon sergeant you have nothing to do.

An anonymous marine recruit

Don't draw fire; it irritates the people around you.

Anonymous

If you see a bomb technician running, try to keep up with him.

USAF Ammo Troop

Bureaucracy

Tim Moore sponsored a resolution in the Texas House of Representatives. He called on the House to commend Albert de Salvo for his unselfish service to 'his country, his state and his community'. The resolution stated that: 'This compassionate gentleman's dedication and devotion to his women has enabled the weak and the lonely throughout the nation to achieve and maintain a new degree of concern for their future. He has been officially recognised by the state of Massachusetts for his noted activities and unconventional techniques involving population control and applied psychology.'

The resolution was passed unanimously.

Representative Moore then revealed that he had only tabled the notion to show that the legislature often passes bills and resolutions without reading them or understanding what they say. Albert Salvo was the Boston Strangler.

I spy
The FBI recently released formerly classified files. Among 15,000 pages newly available to the public were in-depth reports on organised crime and anti-communist groups. There were also several Victoria's Secret catalogues addressed to J. Edgar Hoover.

The wood from the trees
An American senator had a wooden leg. One day, he was in such a terrible hurry that he parked his car on a double yellow line. Hoping to avoid a parking ticket, he wrote a message for the warden on his windscreen: 'Have pity – wooden leg.' He returned to find both a ticket and a note: 'No pity – wooden heart!'

The battle of the bulge
Ted Kennedy has a reputation for enjoying, wine, women and song. In the early 1990s, a member of the paparazzi caught him in a very compromising position with a young lady on a boat off the coast of France. When Ted returned from his 'leisure time' in Europe, one of his Republican opponents in the Senate caustically observed: 'Well, Senator, I see you've changed your position on off-shore drilling.'

In his later years, Ted has put on a lot of weight. One estimate puts him at up to 22 stone. One of his Democratic colleagues observed: 'I see he's finally carrying his weight within the party.'

Caught out
Ted Kennedy tells of a lecturer at a theological college who informed his class that the subject of his next lecture would be the sin of deceit. By way of preparation, he told the class, they should read the 17th chapter of St Mark's Gospel. When the class began, the lecturer asked how many had complied with his instructions. Most of the students raised their hands: 'Thank you,' said the lecturer. 'It is to people like you that today's lecture is especially addressed. There is no 17th chapter in Mark's Gospel.'

A letter

When John F. Kennedy was sent to boarding school he was always thinking of clever ways to try and get money from his father. He once wrote:

Dear Dad,
$chool i$ really great. I am making lot$ of friend$ and $tudying hard. With all my $tuff, I $imply can't think of anything I need, $o if you like, you can ju$t $end me a card, a$ I would love to hear from you.
Love,
Your $on.

The following response arrived a week later:

Dear Son,
I kNOw that astroNOmy, ecoNOmics and oceaNOgraphy are eNOugh to keep even an hoNOurs student busy. Do NOt forget that the pursuit of kNOwledge is a NOble task and you can never study eNOugh.
Love,
Dad.

Elementary

JFK's favourite story was about the time Sherlock Holmes and Dr Watson went on a camping trip. The pair set up their tent and fell asleep. Some hours later, Holmes woke up his faithful friend.

'Watson, look up at the sky and tell me what you see.'

Watson replied, 'I see millions of stars.'

'What does that tell you?'

Watson pondered for a minute. 'Astronomically speaking, it tells me that there are millions of galaxies and potentially billions of planets. Astrologically, it tells me that Saturn is in Leo. Time wise, it appears to be approximately a quarter past three. Theologically, it's evident the Lord is all-powerful and we are small and insignificant. Meteorologically, it seems that we will have a beautiful day tomorrow. What does it tell you?'

Holmes was silent for a moment, then spoke, 'Watson, you idiot, someone has stolen our tent.'

Listen and Learn

Young boy: 'Dad, are caterpillars good to eat?'

John F. Kennedy: 'Don't talk about such things at the dinner table. We'll discuss it later.'

Boy after lunch: 'Never mind, Dad. That caterpillar was on your salad, but he's all gone now.'

Coincidences

Were you aware of the number of coincidences in the biographies of Abraham Lincoln and John F. Kennedy?

Abraham Lincoln was elected to Congress in 1846.
John F. Kennedy was elected to Congress in 1946.

Abraham Lincoln was elected President in 1860.
John F. Kennedy was elected President in 1960.

The names Lincoln and Kennedy each contain seven letters.

Both were particularly concerned with civil rights.
Both wives lost children while living in the White House.

Both Presidents were shot on a Friday.
Both Presidents were shot in the head.

Lincoln's secretary was named Kennedy.
Kennedy's secretary was named Lincoln.

Both were assassinated by Southerners.
Both were succeeded by Southerners.

Both successors were named Johnson.
Andrew Johnson, who succeeded Lincoln, was born in 1808.
Lyndon Johnson, who succeeded Kennedy, was born in 1908.

John Wilkes Booth, who assassinated Lincoln, was born in 1839.
Lee Harvey Oswald, who assassinated Kennedy, was born in 1939.

Both assassins were known by their three names.
Both names are comprised of fifteen letters.

Booth ran from the theatre and was caught in a warehouse.
Oswald ran from the warehouse and was caught in a theatre.

Booth and Oswald were assassinated before their trials.

But here's the clincher…
A week before Lincoln was shot, he was in Monroe, Maryland.
A week before Kennedy was shot, he was in Marilyn Monroe.

The lunatics are running the asylum

Fancy working for this organisation? It has less than 600 employees but:

- 29 have been accused of spousal abuse.
- 7 have been arrested for fraud.
- 19 have been accused of writing bad cheques.
- 117 have bankrupted at least two businesses.
- 3 have been arrested for assault.
- 71 cannot get a credit card because they have bad credit.
- 14 have been arrested on drug-related charges.
- 8 have been arrested for shoplifting.
- 84 were stopped for drink-driving in one year alone.

Can you guess which organisation this is? Give up?
It is the 535-member United States Congress.

A frightening prospect

You might be a Republican if:

- You've tried to argue that poverty could be abolished if people were allowed to keep more of their minimum wage.
- You've ever referred to someone as 'my (insert racial or ethnic minority here) friend'.
- You're a pro-lifer, but support the death penalty.
- You've ever referred to the moral fibre of something.
- You've ever uttered the phrase, 'Why don't we just bomb the sons of bitches'.
- You've ever called a secretary or waitress 'Honey'.
- You don't think *The Simpsons* is all that funny, but you watch it because that Flanders fellow makes a lot of sense.
- You don't let your kids watch *Sesame Street* because you think Bert and Ernie are sexually deviant.
- You use any of these terms to describe your wife: old ball and chain, little woman, old lady, tax credit…
- You argue that you need 300 handguns in case a bear ever attacks your home.
- Vietnam makes a lot of sense to you.
- You've ever called education a luxury.
- You wonder if donations to the Pentagon are tax deductible.
- You own a vehicle with an 'Ollie North: American Hero' sticker.
- You think all artists are gay.
- You've ever urged someone to pull themselves up by their bootstraps, when they don't even have shoes.

Note: If only some of these apply to you relax – you are not a Republican. You are simply a member of the Progressive Democrats.

The Wailing Wall

An American journalist was assigned to the Jerusalem bureau and took an apartment overlooking the Wailing Wall. Every day when she looked out, she saw an old Jewish man praying vigorously. So, the journalist went down and introduced herself to him.

She asked, 'You come every day to the wall. How long have you done that and what are you praying for?' The old man replied, 'I have come here to pray every day for 25 years. In the morning I pray for world peace and then for the brotherhood of man. I go home, have a cup of tea and I come back and pray for the eradication of illness and disease from the earth.'

The journalist was amazed. 'How does it make you feel to come here every day for 25 years and pray for these things?' she asked.

The old man looked at her sadly: 'Like I'm talking to a wall.'

Horse manure

When he was US President, Harry Truman once addressed the Washington Garden Club and kept referring to the 'good manure' that must be used on flowers. Some society ladies later complained to the First Lady Margaret Truman: 'Bess, can't you get the President to say fertiliser instead of manure?'

The First Lady replied, 'Heavens, it took me 25 years to get him to say "manure".'

Actual headlines published in the USA in 2005

- Something Went Wrong in Jet Crash, Expert Says
  (Stating the obvious?)
- Police Begin Campaign to Run Down Jaywalkers
  (Is that not taking things to the extreme?)
- Miners Refuse to Work after Death
  (Seems sensible)
- Juvenile Court to Try Shooting Defendant
  (A novel approach to judiciary)
- War Dims Hope for Peace
  (Stating the bleedin' obvious)
- If Strike Isn't Settled Quickly, It May Last Awhile
  (What insight?)
- Cold Wave Linked to Temperatures
  (Fancy that)

The last words

After many years of illness, it appeared that Ronald Reagan might not pull through. Nancy and the rest of the family were at his side, as well as their minister. Knowing that his time might be short, they asked if there was anything that he wanted before he died. He replied, 'I'd like very much to have Bill and Hillary Clinton at my side before I die.' They were all amazed at this request and several assumed that his mental state was far worse than they suspected. Regardless, they went ahead and forwarded his request to the former first family.

Within hours, Bill and Hillary arrived at Ronald's bedside, courtesy of Air Force One. For a time no one said anything. Both Bill and Hillary were touched and flattered that Ronald asked them to be with him during his final moments. They were also puzzled – they were of different political persuasions and had thrown some barbs in one another's direction over the years. Why not George Bush Sr, George W. Bush or some of Reagan's many Hollywood friends? He had never given the Clintons any indication that he particularly liked either of them.

Finally, Bill spoke up and asked, 'Mr President, why did you choose the two of us to be by your bedside at this critical moment?' Ronald mustered up some strength and said, 'I want to die like Jesus on the cross – between two thieves'.

Re-dick-ulous

After the criticism attracted by his inept response to Hurricane Katrina, Vice President Dick Cheney is trying to soften his image. Nonetheless, his spin doctors have been told never to interrupt him when he is yelling at puppies.

Cheney has a new diplomatic mission. Dubya sent him to Azerbaijan to wish that country's new president good luck in his fight against Harry Potter.

Chapter 19 The Terminator

Arnold Schwarzenegger and his sculpted pecs came to prominence when he won the Mr Universe competition five times. At this point, 'the Austrian Oak', had yet to make it in Hollywood. He blamed his lack of success on his thick Austrian accent. The role of the muscle-popping avenger Conan the Barbarian was made for him, and in 1982 his movie-acting career took off. In recent years, his political ambitions have come to the fore.

Der New 2006 California State Employee Handbook

As Governor of California Arnold Schwarzenegger has issued new guidelines for his employees:

1. Sick days

Ve vill no longer accept a doktor's shtatement as proof of sickness. If you are able to go to the doktor, you are able to come to verk.

2. Personal days

Each employee vill receive 104 personal days a year. Dey are called Saturday and Sunday.

3. Lunch break

Skinny people get 30 minutes for lunch, as dey need to eat more, so that dey can look healthy. Normal size people get 15 minutes for lunch to get a balanced meal to maintain their average figure. Fat people get 5 minutes for lunch, because dat's all der time needed to drink der Shlim Fast.

4. Dress code

It is advised that you come to verk dressed according to your salary. If ve see you vearing a $350 Prada shirt, and carrying a $600 Guicci bag, ve vill asume you are doing vell financially and derefore you do not need a raise. If you dress poorly, you need to learn to manage your money better, so dat you may buy nicer clothes, and derefore you do not need a raise. If you dress in betven, you are right vere you need to be and derefore you do not need a raise.

5. Bereavement leave

Dis is no excuse for missing verk. Dere is notting you can do for dead friends, relatives, or co-verkers. Every effort should be made to have non-employees attend to da arranchments. In rare cases vere employee involvement is necessary, da funeral should be scheduled in da late afternoon. Ve vill be glad to allow you to vork troo your lunch hour and subsequently leave vone hour early.

6. Restroom use

Entirely too much time is being spent in da restroom. Dere is now a shtrict tree-minute time limit in der shtalls. At der end of tree minutes, an alarm vill sound, der toilet paper vill retract, the shtall door vill open and a picture will be taken. After your second offence, your picture vill be posted on der company bulletin board under da 'Chronic Offenders' category.

Tank you for your loyalty to our great shtate. Ve are here to provide a positive employment experience.

Der Governator.

Shock horror

In a bizarre new scandal that could short-circuit Arnold Schwarzenegger's political career, a talking Governator doll has been accused of groping Barbie. The allegations were made at a press conference outside Mattel's Malibu Dream House, where a tearful Barbie – accompanied by a Gloria Allred doll – described a 1977 incident in which a Governator action figure allegedly used his kung-fu grip to grab her chest. A spokesdoll for the Governator, which is manufactured by a Connecticut company, denied Barbie's charges.

However, a seven-week *Times* investigation has uncovered other alleged victims of Governator groping.

'When you press the button that activates the Governator's voice chip, he makes crude remarks,' said one female doll, who requested anonymity. 'He asked if my breasts were real or plastic.'

Governator aides said their boss apologised if he offended anyone, but they blasted their accuser's claims. 'She isn't even anatomically correct,' said Governator aide G.I. Joe. 'There's nothing to grope.'

I'll be back

Arnold Schwarzenegger is not known for his subtlety. When he became Governor of California, he decided to launch a new campaign to ban junk food in schools. He decided to call it: 'No child left with a big behind.'

A date with Fergie

Fergie, the Duchess of York not the football manager, talked about her meeting with JFK Jr. On the subject of Arnold Schwarzenegger he said: 'When my cousin Maria introduced her fiancé, Arnold, to Uncle Ted, she said: "Don't think of him as a Republican, think of him as them as the man I love. And if you can't do that, think of him as the man who could break you in two."'

Arnie has his critics. Robin Williams claimed: 'Arnold Schwarzenegger's acted in plenty of movies but spoke less dialogue than any actor, except maybe Lassie.'

Back to Bach

Stephen Spielberg is making a film about famous composers. Sylvester Stallone, Pierce Brosnan and Arnold Schwarzenegger agreed to take part. Spielberg asked Stallone what role he wanted. Stallone said, 'I will be Mozart.' He asked Brosnan next and the Navan man said, 'Well, Handel first performed his *Messiah* in Dublin. So I should reciprocate his generosity and play him.' Finally, Spielberg turned to Arnold and the big muscle man got up and said menacingly: 'I will be Bach.'

Barbed

Senator Hillary Clinton was attending a party, when she noticed Governor Arnold Schwarzenegger. She walked over to him, and in a quiet voice said: 'If you were my husband I would poison your drink.'

Schwarzenegger smiled, leaned forward, and whispered in her ear, 'If you were my wife I would drink it'.

Word imperfect

Californian Government officials now have to pay a $1 fine when they use a word that is hard for taxpayers to understand. Arnie owes $50,000.

Fair weather friends

Arnie has called a conference on climate change. The Governator is to give the keynote address. His speech will be very short. His exact words will be: 'Fire...hot...bad.'

Chapter 20 Sa-damned

Welcome to Saddam's world. The following compilation provides a graphic and entertaining tour of how one of politics most notorious practitioners pursued personal pleasure. Packed in equal measure are invaluable insights about the war on terror and wry observations about the world's remaining superpower.

When George met Saddam

A week before the war on terror began, Saddam Hussein and George Bush secretly met in Baghdad for talks on sanctions. When George sat down, he noticed that Saddam's chair had three buttons on the armrest. They began talking, but after five minutes Saddam pressed a button and a boxing glove popped out of Bush's chair and bashed him in the face. Bush, barely believing it, carried on talking, but after a few minutes Saddam pressed a second button and out came a large boot and kicked Bush on the shin. George was cheesed off but still remained outwardly calm. They resumed the talks, but after another five minutes, Saddam pressed the final button and from under the table came another boxing glove, which hit Bush right in the groin. Dubya was really fed up and stood up to leave. 'We'll continue this talk next week in the White House,' said the President.

Saddam, choking with laughter, was too proud to say no, so the appointment stood. A week later, Bush received Saddam in the Oval Office, and as Saddam sat down, he saw three buttons in the armrest of Dubya's chair. As the meeting went on, Saddam saw Bush press the first button, and ducked, but nothing happened. This didn't stop Bush from laughing...really loudly. After this, Bush continued where he left off, until he pressed another button. Saddam jumped up and again nothing happened. This time Bush fell out of his chair laughing. Saddam didn't get it – what the hell was happening? But he hadn't been harmed yet, so he sat down again to talk further. After a few minutes Bush pressed the final button. This time, Saddam stayed sitting, but Bush was still rolling on the floor, doubled up with laughter. Saddam was really annoyed by now, so he stood up from his chair and shouted: 'I've had enough of this, I'm going back to Baghdad.'

(Through tears of laughter from the floor): 'Baghdad?…What Baghdad?'

For God's sake

One morning, Saddam Hussein called President Bush and said: 'George, I just called you because I had this incredible dream last night and I had to tell you about it. I could see all of America, and it was peaceful and beautiful and on top of every building, there was a flag.'

Bush asked: 'A flag? What was on the flag?'

Saddam replied: 'Allah is God, God is Allah.'

Bush said: 'You know, Saddam, I'm really glad you called because last night I had a dream, too. I could see all of Baghdad, and there was no more fighting, and it was even more beautiful than before the war; it had been completely rebuilt. And on every building there was a flag.'

Saddam asked: 'George, what was on the flag?'

Bush replied: 'I don't know.'

Saddam said: 'You don't know. Why not?'

Bush replied: 'I never could read Hebrew.'

The American view of Iraq

Q: Why is it twice as easy to train Iraqi fighter pilots?

A: You only have to teach them to take off.

Q: How do you play Iraqi bingo?

A: B-52…F-16…B-2.

Q: What is Iraq's national bird?

A: Duck.

Q: What did Saddam Hussein and General Custer have in common?

A: They both wanted to know where the hell those Tomahawks were coming from.

Q: Why does the Iraqi navy have glass-bottom boats?

A: So they can see their air force.

The TV world according to Saddam

Before Saddam was deposed, the Iraqi prime time television schedule read as follows:

Mondays

8.00	Husseinfeld
8.30	Mad About Everything
9.00	Suddenly Sanctions
9.30	The Bin Laden Show
10.00	Allah McBeal

Tuesdays

8.00	Wheel of Fortune and Terror
8.30	The Price is Right If Saddam says It's Right
9.00	Children Are Forbidden from Saying the Darnedest Things
9.30	Iraq's Wackiest Public Execution Bloopers
10.00	Buffy the Yankee Imperialist Dog Slayer

Wednesdays

8.00	US Military Secrets Revealed
8.30	When Kurds Attack
9.00	Two Guys, A Girl and a Fatwa
9.30	Just Shoot Me
10.00	Veilwatch

Thursday

8.00	Matima loves Chachi
8.30	M*O*U*S*T*A*S*H
9.00	Veronica's Closet Full of Long, Black, Shapeless Dresses
9.30	My Two Baghdads
10.00	Diagnosis: Heresy

Friday

8.00	Everybody Loves Saddam or He'll Have Them Shot
8.30	Only Our Will and Grace from God Can Keep Us from Touching
9.00	Captured Iranian Soldiers Say the Darnedest Things
9.30	Ahmed's Creek
10.00	Desperate Housewives Will Be Shot

On patrol

A squad of American soldiers was patrolling the Iraqi border, when they came across a badly mangled dead body. As they got closer, they found it was an Iraqi soldier.

A short distance up the road, they found a badly mangled American soldier in a ditch, struggling to breathe. They ran to him, cradled his bruised head and asked him what had happened.

'Well,' he whispered, 'I was walking down this road, armed to the teeth when I came across this heavily armed Iraqi border guard. I looked him right in the eye and shouted, 'Saddam Hussein is a moronic, deceitful, lying piece of trash'.

'He looked me right in the eye and shouted back, "George W. Bush is a moronic, deceitful, lying piece of trash too".

'We were standing there shaking hands when the truck hit us.'

Sweet

The US Senate has finally decided to vote on Bush's plans on Iran, without resorting to a filibuster. Dubya was never worried anyway; he thinks a filibuster is a chocolate-covered peanut bar.

Chapter 21 Parish Pump Politics

The following is a list of genuine complaints received by Irish local councils:

- My bush is really overgrown round the front and my back passage has fungus around it.
- …and he's got this huge tool that vibrates the whole house and I just can't take it anymore.
- …it's the dog's mess that I find hard to swallow.
- I want some repairs done to my cooker, as it has backfired and burnt my knob off.
- I wish to complain that my father hurt his ankle very badly when he put his foot in the hole in his back passage.
- …and their 18-year-old son is constantly banging his balls against my fence.
- I wish to report that tiles are missing from the outside toilet roof. I think it was a bad wind the other night that blew them off.
- My lavatory seat is cracked, where do I stand?
- I am writing on behalf of my sink, which is coming away from the wall.
- Will you please send someone to mend the garden path? My wife tripped and fell on it yesterday and she is pregnant. We are getting married in September and we would like it in the garden before we move into the house.
- I request permission to remove my drawers in the kitchen.
- …50 per cent of the walls are damp, 50 per cent have crumbling plaster and the rest are plain filthy.
- I am still having problems with smoke in my new drawers.

- The toilet is blocked and we cannot bath the children until it is cleared.
- Will you please send a man to look at my water? It is a funny colour and not fit to drink.
- Our lavatory seat is broken in half and is now in three pieces.
- Would you please send a man to repair my spout? I am an old-age pensioner and need it badly.
- I want to complain about the farmer across the road; every morning at 6 am his cock wakes me up and it's now getting too much for me.
- The man next door has a large erection in the back garden, which is unsightly and dangerous.
- Our kitchen floor is damp. We have two children and would like a third so please send someone around to do something about it.
- I am a single woman living in a downstairs flat and would you please do something about the noise made by the man I have on top of me every night?
- Please send a man with the right tool to finish the job and satisfy my wife.
- I have had the clerk of the works down on the floor six times but I still have no satisfaction.
- This is to let you know that our lavatory seat is broken and we can't get RTÉ 2.

Conclusion

Every politician should read this:

While walking down the street one day, a female head of state was tragically hit by a car and died. Her soul arrived in heaven and was met by St Peter at the entrance.

'Welcome to Heaven,' said St Peter. 'Before you settle in, it seems there is a problem. We seldom see a high official around these parts, you see, so we're not sure what to do with you.'

'No problem, just let me in,' replied the lady.

'Well, I'd like to but I have orders from higher up. What we'll do is have you spend one day in hell and one in heaven. Then you can choose where to spend eternity.'

'Really, I've made up my mind. I want to be in heaven,' said the head of state.

'I'm sorry but we have our rules.' And with that, St Peter escorted her to the lift and down, down, down she went to hell. The doors opened and she found herself in the middle of a golf course. In the distance was a club and standing in front of it were all her friends and the politicians who had worked with her. Everyone was very happy and in evening dress. They greeted her, hugged her, and reminisced about the good times they had while getting rich at the expense of the people. They played a friendly game of golf and then dined on lobster. Also present was the Devil. He was a very friendly guy who enjoyed dancing and telling jokes. They were having such a good time that, before she realised it, it was time to go. Everyone gave her a big hug and waved while the lift went up. The lift reopened in heaven where St Peter was waiting for her.

'Now it's time to visit heaven.' So 24 hours passed with the head of state joining a large number of contented souls moving from cloud to cloud, playing the harp and singing. Before she realised it, the 24 hours had gone by and St Peter returned: 'Well then, you've spent a day in hell and another in heaven. Now choose your eternal destination.'

She reflected for a minute, then the head of state answered: 'Well, I would never have expected it. I mean heaven has been delightful, but I think I would be better off in hell.'

So St Peter escorted her to the lift and she went down, down, down to hell. The doors opened and she was in the middle of a barren land covered with rubbish. She saw all her friends, dressed in rags, picking up the rubbish and putting it in bags. The Devil came over to her and laid his arm on her neck.

'I don't understand,' stammered the head of state. 'Yesterday I was here and everyone was on the golf course and we ate lobster and danced and had a great time. Now it is a wasteland full of rubbish and my friends look miserable.'

The Devil looked at her, smiled and said, 'Yesterday we were campaigning. Today you voted for us!'